DATE DUE

1 8 2005

Mambisas

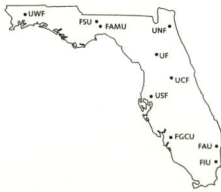

UNIVERSITY PRESS OF FLORIDA / STATE UNIVERSITY SYSTEM

Florida A&M University, Tallahassee
Florida Atlantic University, Boca Raton
Florida Gulf Coast University, Ft. Myers
Florida International University, Miami
Florida State University, Tallahassee
University of Central Florida, Orlando
University of Florida, Gainesville
University of North Florida, Jacksonville
University of South Florida, Tampa
University of West Florida, Pensacola

Mambisas

▲▽▲▽▲▽▲▽▲▽▲▽▲▽▲▽▲▽▲▽▲

Rebel Women in Nineteenth-Century Cuba

Teresa Prados-Torreira

University Press of Florida

Gainesville Tallahassee Tampa Boca Raton
Pensacola Orlando Miami Jacksonville Ft. Myers

10 09 08 07 06   05 6 5 4 3 2 1

A record of cataloging-in-publication data is available
from the Library of Congress.

ISBN 0-8130-2852-3

The University Press of Florida is the scholarly publishing agency
for the State University System of Florida, comprising Florida A&M University,
Florida Atlantic University, Florida Gulf Coast University, Florida International
University, Florida State University, University of Central Florida,
University of Florida, University of North Florida, University
of South Florida, and University of West Florida.

University Press of Florida
15 Northwest 15th Street
Gainesville, FL 32611-2079
http://www.upf.com

A Adrián, Diego y Eloy

▲▼▲▼▲

Contents

Illustrations

Acknowledgments

Any historian working with Cuban sources these days will have encountered this contradiction: there are few places where it is as difficult as in Cuba to do research—because of the limitations imposed by the American embargo, the Cuban bureaucracy, technical obstacles—and few places where librarians and scholars are as generous and helpful.

My guardian angel in Cuba has been Nancy Machado at the José Martí National Library (Biblioteca Nacional José Martí). From helping me find information in Havana to scanning documents and e-mailing them to Chicago, Nancy has been instrumental in allowing me to finish this book. In the process, she has become a dear friend.

I am also very thankful for the friendship and support of Emilio Hernández and Ana Cairo, both of whom, in typical Cuban fashion, have generously shared with me their vast knowledge of Cuban literature and history.

I owe a special debt to three generations of the Mendieta family. I could not have asked for a better introduction to Cuban culture than the one I got through my friendship with Raquel "Kaky" Mendieta when she lived in Chicago. Her death was a painful blow to all her friends. I enjoyed the hospitality of her parents, Raquelito and Tata, in Varadero and benefited from the family's first-rate private library in Havana. The Mendieta house in Playa has become a second home to me, thanks to the generosity of Kaky's son, Horacio "Uky," and his wife, Naylin. It is a true joy to spend time with them, their neighbors, and their friends.

I want to thank my institution, Columbia College Chicago, for its financial support. Research trips, a sabbatical, and copy editing were all financed by the college. I could not have written this book without it.

I want to thank Craig Aaron for helping me edit the first draft of this book. Amy Gorelick, acquisitions editor at the University Press of Florida, and Susan Albury, project editor, have been a pleasure to work with. Verene Sheperd kindly read an early version of this work and pointed out the need to broaden my analysis to include nonpolitical forms of resistance. Kirwin Shaffer made numerous helpful suggestions and encouraged me to strengthen my theoretical framework, and for that I am truly grateful.

I especially want to thank my family for their warm support and encouragement.

Introduction

The island of Cuba was one of the first pieces of land in the Americas occupied by the Spanish. It would become the colony that Spain fought hardest and longest to keep. Throughout the second half of the nineteenth century—and after four hundred years in the hands of the Spanish Crown—Cuba revolted against colonial rule. Despite their paltry military resources, the Cuban rebels were able to keep the well-equipped and experienced Spanish army at bay, thanks largely to the support of the island's population. The Cuban insurgency spanned more than thirty years, with the tension between Spain and the rebel movement peaking in the Ten Years War (1868–1878) and the War of Independence (1895–1898).

Reporter James O'Kelly, who covered the Cuban rebellion in 1869 for the New York *Herald*, used the word *Mambí* to describe to his American readers the territory freed from Spain's control by the Cuban fighters: "The land of the Mambí is to the world a shadow-land, full of doubts and unrealities. It is a legend, and yet a fact. It is called by many names, yet few know where it begins or ends its frontier. Spaniards call it the *manigua*, or Los Montes, Americans talk of it as Free Cuba, and those who dwell within its confines, Cuba Libre, or the Mambi-Land."[1]

Mambí was the name not only of the rebel territory but also of the men—and women—who fought there. The origin of the term remains unclear. The most accepted theory assumes that it is a deformation of *mbi*, a common prefix in Yoruba, the West African language spoken by many Cuban slaves. The Spanish soldiers, unaccustomed to that letter combination, came up with the word *Mambí* to refer pejoratively to the Cuban rebels. The African-sounding epithet was meant to evoke the ample presence of black fighters among the insurgents. Adopted as a badge of honor by the rebels, the name was widely used throughout the anticolonial wars.[2]

In 1869, at the beginning of the Ten Years War, the Cuban rebels gathered in Guáimaro, a small town in eastern Cuba, to convene the First Constitutional Assembly of the Cuban Republic. Ana Betancourt, the wife of one of the opposition leaders, asked to speak on behalf of women. Like Abigail Adams, who, on the eve of the American Revolution in 1776, asked her husband John Adams to "remember the ladies" and extend to them the rights of the young republic, Ana Betancourt wanted the leaders of the Cuban rebellion to include the female population in their vision of a free Cuba. The insurrection was attempting to break the chains that class and race had forged, she told the assembly, and she expressed her hope that the war would also help bring down oppression based on gender and "unpin women's wings."[3]

Ana Betancourt was one of the many Cuban women—black and white, rich and poor, rural and urban—who fought against Spain's colonial rule on the island. These rebels were known as Mambisas, and they became symbols of Cuba's struggle for freedom, a symbol so powerful it continues to be heralded today.[4]

Early signs of women's political activity on the island can be found in the actions that female slaves took to fend off their masters' power, including their participation in slave revolts.[5] Although opposition to slavery only occasionally reached the level of political articulation and organization a revolt required, the records are filled with examples of slave women who subverted the social order by running away, complaining to the authorities about the sale of a relative, or refusing to follow the master's or mistress's instructions.

Free women also had a tradition of social involvement from which to draw. Sherry Johnson, who has studied eighteenth-century Cuba extensively, shows how the island's position as a military post forced women to take the reins of their households and businesses on the many occasions when the men were on military duty. Especially vocal were the *limosneras* (women seeking alms), a group of several hundred women who demanded from the government the benefits and pensions to which they were entitled as the widows of officers and soldiers who had served the Crown in Florida, before Spain lost it to Britain in 1763.[6]

The transformation of Cuba from an unstable military post in the 1700s to a wealthy plantation society in the early 1800s had a direct impact on women. When families benefited from the more stable rhythm of civilian life and the men no longer needed to rely on their wives' help to keep their businesses going, women lost whatever legal and economic power that they had enjoyed, if only sporadically. The new ideal of femininity portrayed women as angelic and passive. But this ornamental position had some advantages. With the new affluence came a gradual expansion of women's educational opportunities, and a greater exposure to attitudes and ideas that celebrated individualism and questioned traditional mores.

The flourishing of the slave system also meant exponential growth in the number of Cubans of African descent. This segment of the population would play a crucial role in helping develop a distinct identity for the island.

By the early 1800s, a rift was growing between those who pledged allegiance to Madrid and those who thought Cuba had needs the colonial power could not fulfill. Women contributed to marking this division and strengthening anticolonial sentiment in numerous ways. Throughout the second half of the century, spurred by the vision of a free Cuba, Cuban women's involvement intensified until, in the 1890s, it reached the level of a mass movement. The wars turned largely uneducated women with limited political experience into savvy and passionate political players. Their collective work was crucial to the survival of the rebel army. They staffed makeshift hospitals and war supply centers; they worked as messengers and undercover agents; they organized fund-raising activities to buy weapons; they joined revolutionary clubs; they wrote pamphlets, hid ammunition, and even shot enemy soldiers and rose through military ranks.

But wars are not fought only on the battlefield. In the home, the square, the street, the country road, the hidden *conuco* (a small garden or field next to a humble dwelling), thousands of women took a political stand. Within their families and their communities, women created a climate that celebrated Cuban nationalism and helped shape a new society. The Cuban insurgency was as much a battle of ideas as of bullets, its scope reaching far beyond the struggle to put an end to a colonial government.

Throughout the first half of the 1800s, two opposing world views came into conflict: one fought to maintain the hierarchical social order the ancien régime had carved, where monarchies ruled, the church was prominent, and colonies served the interests of their home country; the other embraced liberalism and its defense of democracy, individual autonomy, a free market, secularism, and technological innovations. This tension was present not only in the colonies but also in Spain, where the contest between absolutism and constitutionalism resulted in periodic crises and changes of government. Few voices, however, were heard in Spain, even among the most liberal quarters, that demanded that democratic rights be extended to the colonies, since that would have prevented the country from reaping the economic benefits the colonial relationship provided.

Spain's defense of the status quo in Cuba was applauded by Cuba's wealthy classes, particularly by the plantation owners, who feared a slave revolt might follow the defeat of the Spanish army. And yet, these same men realized that slavery was an anachronism and that, if they were going to have an economic future at all, it lay with a capitalist, free-market society.

A parallel ambivalence in regard to slavery existed among the insurgents. When they rose against Spain in 1868, their political vision, similar to that of America's Founding Fathers in 1776, reconciled both the exaltation of freedom and the acceptance of, or at least tolerance for, slavery. It would take arduous negotiations before the rebel government adopted the abolition of slavery as its cause.

Yet for all its contradictions, the Cuban insurgency sought to erode the values on which the ancien régime was built, including the practice of enforced labor. For inspiration, the rebels dipped into the rich political culture of their age. They were conversant with the Enlightenment ideals of the American and the French revolutions, yet they relied on the transcendent and emotional rhetoric of the romantics; they adopted the defense of freedom and individualism found in liberalism and shared the concern for justice that characterized the turbulent working-class movement of the 1800s.

My study examines the many forms in which women undermined traditional forms of authority and thus helped foster a revolutionary climate. Scholars of nationalism like to stress that nations are the product of a determined group of people who successfully create a sense of collective identity. In other words, nations are what Benedict Anderson has characterized as "imagined communities."[7] That view does not attempt to question the validity of the nationalist claim. As Anne McClintock has pointed out, "Nations are not simply phantasmagoria of the mind, but are historical practices through which social difference is both invented and performed."[8] The nineteenth century was a time for Cuba to imagine itself as an entity separate from Spain, a time for Cubans to both highlight existing social practices and create new ones that differentiated them from the colonial power. Antonio Gramsci's notion of counterhegemony is useful to this discussion in that it helps describe the active role women played in conjuring up an alternative world view. According to Gramsci, subordinate groups can, at times, change their society's dominant culture by introducing a new set of assumptions that has appeal to a large segment of their society.[9] Nineteenth-century Cuban women's determined support for the rebel cause contributed to solidifying the notion that stepping outside the legal system was not only acceptable but heroic. They were instrumental in the creation of ideas that directly or indirectly challenged the status quo. As transmitters and producers of values, as keepers of tradition, Cuban women played a significant role in building a Cuban sense of identity.

In the rebels' iconography, women occupied a prominent place, their courage often invoked to inspire the fighters. For how could Cuban soldiers hesitate to give their lives for the insurgency when their mothers, their sisters, their daughters were willing to do so? This study pays attention to the Mambisa image the rebels crafted in order to promote the cause of war—an image that highlighted the women's self-sacrificing and accommodating spirit. The portrait of rebel women as "obedient daughters" is not wholly inaccurate. For many, their involvement was directly related to identification with their male relatives, particularly in the early stages of the rebellion. But there is also ample evidence of women who stepped beyond the comfortable confines of the official rebel rhetoric to take a leading role in defining the very terms of the rebellion, thus creating tensions and contradictions in the insurgent society.

Nationalist symbols, for obvious reasons, cannot be subtly layered. Rebel culture portrayed the Mambisas as a unified lot and celebrated women's commitment to the patriotic cause, no matter their background. However, scholars interested in the female experience have been careful not to group all women into a single category, reminding us to be sensitive to factors such as class, race, and religion, which make women's experiences distinct. This warning is highly relevant. The disparities in Cuban women's war experience mirror the vast socioeconomic differences of their society. Opposition to the government could not affect a wealthy woman and a slave in the same ways. Yet one remarkable aspect of this story is that women of various backgrounds crossed paths as often as they did and fought with the common goal of helping the rebel army challenge Spain's domination.

In her perceptive study on the mulatto woman (*mulata*) as an iconic figure in nineteenth-century Cuban literature, Vera Kutzinski points out that black and white women have traditionally been portrayed as embodying opposite characteristics: black women as sensual and licentious; white women as cold and proper.[10] Examining the Mambisas' ordeal helps us look beyond this stereotypical dualism and draw a richer, more complex portrait of the island's women.

Also in the last few decades, feminist theorists have raised the question of whether women's past is so notably different from men's past that telling women's story might require discarding conventional categories to capture it, developing its own language to describe it.[11] Did Cuban women experience the rebellion against Spain in such a distinct way that a conventional chronology to tell their story is ineffective? Unquestionably, the Mambisas' war experience was different from the men's. Women only occasionally joined the actual fighting. Furthermore, the project of a free Cuba only tangentially encompassed a renegotiation of gender roles within the family and in the larger society. For men, notions of progress and independence had a personal, immediate dimension; the meaning for women was more ambiguous.

Yet one crucial characteristic element of the Cuban conflict is how closely men and women shared this ordeal. Extended families and communities of neighbors, entire towns, jointly experienced the dangers and tribulations of their political involvement. For this reason, I have found it fitting to rely on a traditional chronology to frame the Mambisas' story. Cuba's fight against colonialism shows that gender is, as feminist theorists like to point out, a fluid concept best understood not as an essential part of one's identity but as a performance that varied according to the circumstances, a flexible tenet that could be redefined in times of social turmoil.[12] Just as it had with class and race barriers, the war offered women a chance to cross gender conventions and to perform or behave "in a manly way," an opportunity many found liberating. As the Mambisas explored what it meant to be Cuban, they also searched for a new definition of womanhood.

My study analyzes how the Mambisas' rebellion, their actions, ideas, writing, and public gestures, intentionally and unintentionally, willingly and unwillingly, helped Cubans achieve political adulthood. How did women's involvement in the anticolonial cause, and the way the popular imagination portrayed this involvement, contribute to the molding of a national character? How did their challenge to authority help create a revolutionary identity for the Cuban people while also redefining the feminine ideal?

I am interested in understanding what compelled these women to take an active stance in the wars. What moved them to risk their well-being and that of their families? What did the concept of Free Cuba (Cuba Libre) mean to them, a segment of the population that was disenfranchised even under the insurgents' legal system—"their being both of and not of the nation?"[13]

Unraveling the enigma of the Mambisa poses a challenge. The heavily patriotic historiography of the republican period turned rebel women into characters stiff with Spartan virtues. As Lynn Stoner has discussed, politicians and writers of this period used the Mambisa image to help restore national pride. The women were portrayed as honorable martyrs, their stories hardly distinguishable from each other.[14]

Treatment of rebel women by Marxist historians has been equally formulaic. Aline Helg, who has studied the participation of Afro-Cubans in Cuba's independence project, argues that the dominance of Marxism-Leninism in Cuban historiography has limited the discussion of race.[15] The same could be said about women. Marxist historians interpret the anticolonial struggle as the beginning of a triumphant march toward a national destiny that was fulfilled by the 1959 Revolution. Anything obstructing the realization of the revolutionary ideal was, at best, a distraction, at worst, a betrayal of the Cuban cause. Women's participation in the fight for a free Cuba is highly commended by these scholars, but only in the sense that it contributed to the greater revolutionary cause. Thus, any contradictions that gender might have generated have been obliterated.

I am interested in looking beyond the façade of the brave matron to see what can be discovered about the actual thoughts and feelings of these, indeed, brave women. To that purpose, I have relied as much as possible on the firsthand accounts left by the women themselves. These are more numerous than one might expect. Autobiographies, diaries, letters, essays, and newspaper articles are the foundation of this study. Since I am particularly interested in women's contribution in the realm of cultural values, I have also found it relevant to include poetry and works of fiction by and about women. Unless I indicate otherwise, I use my own translations.

Although there are notable exceptions, resources addressing the participation of poor, and often black, women are less common than the traces left by their middle-class counterparts. I have tried to incorporate as many references to these anonymous rebels as I could find.

Chronologically, my study lies between Sherry Johnson's analysis of eighteenth-century Cuban women and Lynn Stoner's work on the island's feminism in the early decades of the twentieth century. Johnson sees a continuity between the independent-minded Cuban woman of the 1700s and the Mambisas of the 1800s.[16] I, however, emphasize the political differences between the two groups. The Mambisas are unique because they helped define the meaning of *cubanidad* (Cubanness), just as their ties with Spain were crucial to the identity of previous generations of white women. Nevertheless, I take to heart

Johnson's warning not to find "rebellion and resistance where little to none existed."[17] The struggle for independence was a road filled with ambivalence and contradictions. Characterizing most Cuban women as rebel fighters would be a distortion of reality. Furthermore, many rebel women and men traced their family roots to Spain, often removed from the peninsula only by one or two generations. While their participation in the birth of a new society implied a rejection of their ancestors' values, a deeply embedded Spanish culture continued to shape their daily views and actions. The fragile reconciliation of various heritages and ideals, the unresolved tension between change and tradition, shaped, with women's help, twentieth-century Cuba's national identity.

Only a minority of the women I study were specifically concerned with the expansion of women's rights. But whether or not they were interested in feminist ideals, the Mambisas' political activism contributed to setting the stage for the twentieth-century Cuban women's movement.

In addition to Johnson and Stoner, many scholars have paved the way for my study. Nancy Hewitt's and Paul Estrade's research on Cuban women in exile has been truly helpful. I have also benefited from Verena Martínez-Alier (Stolcke's) work on marriage and race and Rebecca Scott's study of emancipation. The work of Aline Helg and Ada Ferrer, both of whom have studied race in nineteenth-century Cuba, has helped me clarify many ideas.

I owe a debt to many Cuban historians, writers, and reporters who, mostly in the first half of the twentieth century, left brief biographical sketches of a number of Mambisas. The Colección Facticia Faustino García at the José Martí National Library got me started on this quest. Among historians writing in socialist Cuba, the work of Nydia Sarabia, the biographer of pivotal Mambisas such as Mariana Grajales, has been most helpful. More recently, the works of both Digna Castañeda and Maria del Carmen Barcia on slave women are noteworthy for their rigor and originality.

Although they approach their subjects from different directions—one emphasizing the lasting Spanish influence on Cuban culture, the other, the American impact—the syntheses of both Manuel Moreno Fraginals and Louis Pérez helped me frame the story I wanted to tell.[18]

Chapters 1 and 2 give an overview of women's regular life patterns, growing out of their racial and social background, and explore the roots of both black and white women's support for the rebellion. Chapter 3 analyzes women's contributions—still largely of a symbolic nature—to the growing anticolonial sentiment in the prewar years. Chapter 4 examines the Mambisas' involvement in the Ten Years War, both as active participants and as iconic symbols of the rebel rhetoric. Chapter 5 focuses on two prominent Mambisas—Emilia Casanova and Ana Betancourt—during this conflict. Chapter 6 examines women's activities in the 1880s and the early 1890s, in other words, the years between the two military conflicts; Chapter 7 discusses women's role in the War of Independence. Finally, Chapter 8 analyzes how the American media used one Cuban woman, Evangelina Cossío Cisneros, to promote the cause of war. I hope to have added a new layer to the subject of Evangelina Cisneros by including Cuban sources not yet used by other historians, which further demonstrate the manipulation of gender notions for military purposes.

Much of the existing Cuban historiography on the subject of Mambisas has a laundry-list quality. The reader is confronted with innumerable names of women who took part in the rebellion, but with scant information on the significance of their role. I have tried to limit my analysis to either women whose participation I consider extraordinary or women whose actions exemplify those taken by many others. Unavoidably, I could not mention many remarkable Mambisas. I am confident that in the coming years more historians will be drawn to the lives and stories of these rebels.

1

▲▼▲▼▲

The Hammock

Bound by Privilege

Nineteenth-century characterizations of Cuban ladies are not flattering. Foreign visitors often commented on the women's indolence, reporting that all they did was lounge in a hammock, a cup of chocolate in one hand and a cigarette in the other. In 1885, a reporter for the New York *Figaro* described the island's daughters as lazy, frivolous, ignorant dolls who never engaged in any productive activity.[1] Spanish writer Raimundo Cabrera was no more forgiving. Referring to the Cuban woman of comfortable means, he wrote: "She neglects domestic work and is only fit to lie in a hammock and fan herself."[2]

These comments, though a caricature, do contain elements of truth. Affluent women enjoyed a slow-paced, leisurely life, since their slaves attended to the most strenuous domestic duties. Excluded from the worlds of work and politics and limited in their artistic and cultural contributions to minor, ornamental gestures, the women of the Creole bourgeoisie spent a great deal of time doing very little, for there was little for them to do.

In *Cecilia Valdés* (1879), a novel that vividly captures nineteenth-century Cuban society, Cirilo Villaverde pokes fun at the ladies' passivity. Yet, as an insider, he understood that inactivity did not prevent women from closely supervising their domestic world. Doña Rosa, one of the novel's main characters, runs a household that includes a small army of slaves and servants.

Every morning, she sits comfortably back in a dining room armchair with a cup of *café con leche*. From this vantage point, she keeps a keen eye on her subordinates' work. Have the laundresses finished the washing and ironing? Are the dressmakers wasting time talking? Have the coachmen adequately cleaned the carriages? And that slave sent on an errand, has he come back? She asked the doorman to make a pair of shoes for another slave while he guarded the door; are they finished? The cook was told the night before to go to market early; has he brought back the provisions she ordered?[3]

Only those who belonged to the island's economic elite, however, lived such an easy existence. Family obligations and household management called most Cuban women away from armchairs and hammocks to play an active role as wives, mothers, and grandmothers. The average white mistress owned but a handful of slaves. The slaves helped alleviate the hardships of domestic life, but they did not completely free white women from household work in a society where families, often large, were still self-sufficient in many regards.

Cuban women inhabited a small universe bounded by tradition and domesticity. While men traveled freely around the island and abroad, women spent most of their time at home. Men were educated about the world, while women's education was narrow and limited. Too much knowledge was deemed dangerous, unfeminine. Innocence, a precious feminine virtue, was thought to survive only if women were kept in a state of ignorance. Until the early nineteenth century, even writing was suspect. After all, a woman who could write could communicate with a lover. Before then, women were taught only embroidery, prayers, and some general notions of etiquette.[4]

By the 1820s, however, girls' education had expanded considerably. The affluent classes began to send their daughters to private academies or religious schools, such as those run by the Ursuline nuns. There the girls learned penmanship, geography and history, basic French, some music, grammar, arithmetic, and, of course, embroidery and prayers.[5] At the end of the school year, parents and relatives were invited to admire the girls' progress—their emphatic readings; the array of handkerchiefs, lace, shirts, and tapestries they had produced; and how well they had memorized their prayers.[6]

According to British consul David Turnbull, who studied the state of education on the island in the 1840s, fewer than 10 percent of white Cuban girls attended primary school at that time. The percentage was even smaller for free black girls in cities, who were regularly excluded from both private and public schools, as were peasants—black and white. Of course, no schools were available to slave children.[7]

Although nineteenth-century public schools for girls were few and disorganized, efforts increasingly were made to regulate instruction, as seen in a growing number of publications addressing this matter. Official textbooks for educating girls in the public school system combined moral lessons and practical advice on domestic economy. One textbook reads: "Resignation in a woman is essential, since there is not a moment of her life when she is not made aware of her inferiority to the opposite sex. And if, instead of yielding to this fate, she should insist on pursuing her goals, what would she gain from this unequal match but a shameful defeat, a belated sense of despair, contempt, and abandonment?"[8]

How much knowledge was appropriate for a woman? One textbook concludes, neither too much nor too little: "A woman who barely knows how to read and count is just as displeasing in society as one who seeks to master all of the sciences."[9] In no way should girls' education turn them into philosophers or writers, vocations incompatible with their duties as wives and mothers. It was important, a guide advised, for women to learn how to read with expression, to develop good handwriting and some understanding of arithmetic. Geography and history were important, too, because they could come in handy at social gatherings. But girls should be taught only historical events from which a moral lesson could be learned, so as not to corrupt their views. Novels were considered a waste of time. Dancing was acceptable under strict supervision, but drawing was better, particularly of flowers and landscapes, subjects more appropriate for a woman's gaze than the human body.

The most significant aspect of a woman's education was religious instruction. Religion taught women to conform to the feminine model society expected of them. Piety, resignation, and charity were feminine virtues religious instruction helped transmit and affirm. So was modesty. As one girls' textbook puts it: "There is NO more horrible object in the human species than a woman without modesty."[10]

Maintaining a girl's modesty was so important that any activity that could jeopardize it—including learning too much or being exposed to new sights, people, or ideas—was to be avoided. Fearing that a girl's innocence could be corrupted, parents took their daughters out of school as soon as they reached puberty and, in the best-case scenario, continued their education with a private tutor at home.[11] Anselmo Suárez y Romero, writer and pedagogue, complained to his contemporaries about this practice in an article on the incomplete education of Cuban women:

Those girls could swiftly and accurately point out places on a map; those girls could solve arithmetic problems with hardly a mistake; those girls could write elegantly and with ease; those girls could speak in foreign languages; they could paint landscapes and play the piano; and recite historical events fairly confidently; and they could define, though vaguely, the immense duties of the fair sex. But it seems to you, who are obliged to toil without respite on their behalf, that they already know enough, and should you admit to removing them prematurely from their schools, you claim not to do so for ignoble reasons but because here young ladies of a certain age cannot be far from the protective mother's wing, which shelters them from all dangers.[12]

Aurelia Castillo, a writer from Camagüey, was able to overcome her limited education and have a significant presence in the cultural life of the island. She was born in 1842 to a middle-class family. As a child, she received private lessons from a tutor until he was forced into exile for his political views. She then had to rely on her own guidance and her friends' support, a predicament characteristic of largely self-taught Cuban females. Reflecting on her education in a letter to a friend, she wrote: "I have read a lot," then scratched out "a lot" and wrote "some." "Knowing my inclination, all my friends gave me books as presents and lent me books and newspapers." Inspired by her mother's love for poetry, she wrote her first sonnet, one with a political undertone, when she was just a teenager.[13]

During the long hours adolescent girls stayed at home after leaving school, they, like Aurelia Castillo, entertained themselves with poetry, music, and needlepoint.[14] Social occasions kept life interesting: trips to picturesque sites in the country; military band concerts; and parties with friends and relatives, where young people had an opportunity to meet and dance with the opposite sex. At these gatherings, women could be expressive, charming, and loquacious, but at no time could their innocence and purity be open to question.

Men and women were held to widely different moral standards. Unfaithfulness in a man was expected and tolerated—in a woman, it was inexcusable. In fact, women's lives were organized around guarding their reputation and honor. The most important lesson they learned was to fear public opinion and to respect social conventions. In the early 1800s, strict standards of modesty dictated that women wear dresses long enough to cover their shoes. Proper women never ventured out in public by themselves. Female teachers, for instance, had a male relative accompany them to and from school. Class, race, and gender determined who belonged in the streets. It was a white man's privilege to move freely beyond the household, and a white woman's privilege not to do so. They sent their slaves back and forth to the stores with this or that request. Black females, with no reputation to safeguard, could wander in and out of their homes without a male escort. "There are no women walking in the streets, except negresses," noted an American traveler.[15] Another traveler observed: "A woman of respectability is scarcely ever seen walking in the streets unless she is a foreigner, or of the lower class, such as seller of fruit, etc."[16]

The only time the streets were not off limits for white women of comfortable means was when they were riding in a carriage, an exception that allowed the wives and daughters of the respectable classes a certain degree of mobility and freedom. In Havana and other towns, the most popular form of entertainment for affluent women was the daily ride in the family's *volante*, the horse carriage of nineteenth-century Cuba, later replaced by the *quitrín*, a more stable model. The carriage took the ladies to their favorite shops and to see and be seen on the fashionable *paseos* (boulevards). In *Cecilia Valdés*, Villaverde writes:

> As long as they didn't go on foot or to pay a formal call, it was quite possible for two or even three young ladies to cover the entire city, do their shopping, chat with the young Spaniards in the shops, and, at night, attend the concerts in the Plaza de Armas or the Alameda de Paula and receive the homage and adoration that their friends and lovers paid them from the steps of the carriage. However, even to pay a visit on foot in the vicinity of her home, a young Cuban woman was required by society to be accompanied, if not by a relative, then by a slave.[17]

Mercedes Santa Cruz y Montalvo, Countess of Merlín, a Cuban aristocrat and writer, commented on well-to-do Havana ladies' abhorrence of setting foot on the streets. After their evening ride through the fashionable boulevards, the ladies stopped in front of the commercial establishments of their choice and, without leaving their carriage, the articles they were interested in were brought to them for inspection. "This way the ladies of Havana wind their way through the city, from six o'clock to midnight, never setting foot on the ground."[18]

Despite the pressure to display a most modest behavior, young Cuban women, like women in any other society, found ways to break rules and stretch restrictions. The Countess of Merlín describes how young women flirted with their lovers: "Her heart beats faster, her pulse accelerates as she listens intently for the slightest sound from within the house where Mama is taking a siesta. With clever forethought, the girl has left her needles and embroidery in plain view on the sewing table, so that if she were to hear her mother's step she could instantly appear to be working diligently. It has been a false alarm. She returns to her seat by the window to await the arrival of the young student who will brave the midday sun to come running at the prearranged signal."[19]

Cuban women married at a very young age, fifteen or sixteen, when they were still little more than girls. A strict array of social rules surrounded the behavior of a woman who was about to marry. Early in the century, public custom demanded that a young bride not be seen in public one week before or after the wedding. Dolores María Ximeno's grandmother grew up in Matanzas, in a house of "big mirrors, mahogany frames, silk curtains, marble shelves, and bronze lamps filled with candles changed every night."[20] She told her granddaughter how, on a day preceding her wedding, she went out on the balcony to see a procession passing. Her grandmother, scandalized, ordered her to come inside immediately, reminding her that she was *amonestada*; in other words, her marriage banns had been published, and thus it was impudent to be seen in public.[21]

As the nineteenth century progressed, the severity of social norms defining women's behavior softened, thanks to factors that had been at work since the late 1700s. The Enlightenment's emphasis on reason and progress had captured the Spanish colonies' imagination and influenced the views of Cuba's educated classes. In the early 1800s, under the aegis of liberalism, the spirit of freedom swept the American continent, challenging the ideological dominance of the Catholic Church and signaling the beginning of a new era of secular values.

Equally significant were economic changes. When Cuba prospered and moved from its position as a struggling colony to the world's foremost sugar producer, the importance of female modesty and purity diminished, replaced by a more frivolous image of femininity. The wives and daughters of the island's big property owners and tradesmen lived in a world of luxury paid for by fabulous sugar profits. Their mansions, dresses, and carriages became unquestionable evidence of the head of the household's success. The Christian morality that until then had ruled Cuban women's lives now had to compete with a growing mercantilist spirit, which rewarded charm and beauty rather than piety and modesty. José María de Heredia's short story "Economía femenil" ["Feminine Economy"](1829) pokes fun at this new extravagance. In this story, a man comments on the alarming expenses incurred by his young wife,

Eugenia. She is quick to retort that he has no reason to complain: "My shoes last me a week and my gloves I can wear twice. Furthermore, I don't ruin you with the weekly expenses or with bills from the dressmaker or the hairdresser, nor do I ask you for new furniture every year; I go to the theater only four days a week; I never gamble, and my daily dress is a simple frock of printed calico or muslin; and a hat lasts me a month."[22]

Despite the differences between the early emphasis on female modesty and the later celebration of female beauty, the two positions were built on a common ground. The emerging commercial mentality continued to portray women as subordinate, but now there was a new emphasis on individualism that women could use to their advantage.

While parents continued to arrange their daughters' marriages well into the nineteenth century, young women were increasingly able to make their opinions known and could dismiss suitors they found unpleasant. Throughout the 1800s, romantic literature and sensibility dominated the island's cultural scene. The work of romantic authors such as George Sand, Shelley, Lord Byron, Walter Scott, Goethe, and Manzoni could be found in the well-stocked libraries of the Cuban middle class. Although only the more liberal-minded parents allowed their daughters to read such work, these authors influenced minor Cuban writers, who produced hundreds of romantic novels with a female audience in mind. These novels affirmed the role of women as angelic and domestic, but also encouraged women to give priority to their own sentiments and sense of independence. Romanticism allowed women to imagine themselves as the object, as well as the subject, of passionate love.

Reflecting this new sensibility was the popularity of "albums" among Cuban women. Fashionable in European cities like Paris and Madrid, the album was a small bound book in which a woman collected artistic tributes, in most cases produced by men. Poems, stories, musical pieces, photographs, miniatures, and flattering sentences were carefully collected to create an album, a process that could take years. Combining formality and passion, male writers fashioned in these albums an image of womanhood that was both innocent and alluring. Women were compared to birds, butterflies, and flowers. They were queens of love, their beauty and sensuality true muses to the writer's inspiration.[23]

Romanticism also allowed women to express their own desires and longings through poetry. Women's love poems, while relying on a male erotic vocabulary, were often dedicated to another woman. A good example is young poet Juana Borrero's rhyme to a female friend:

Down your morbid back
your blond hair unbraids;
it allows to spread rebellious
the torrent of fire
over your turgid breast
and the marble of your neck![24]

Romanticism promoted contradictory expectations for women. The movement's exaltation of freedom and passion encouraged them to seek their own identity as individuals. At the same time, the romantic portrayal of women as ethereal and ornamental reaffirmed their subordination. Luisa Pérez de Zambrana, a writer from Oriente better known for her poetry, captures the tension women felt as they tried to meet their needs while living up to the romantic ideal. In her novel *Angélica y Estrella*, which was serialized between 1864 and 1876, she follows the conventional nineteenth-century formula of contrasting two young women. Estrella is beautiful and captivating, but also frivolous and flirtatious. Angélica, her cousin, though not so striking, is, as her name suggests, an angel who embodies nineteenth-century female virtues. She is spiritual, pious, humble, sweet, delicate, and modest. Through the character of the bad cousin, Estrella, however, the writer allows herself to express what sound like her own doubts about women's roles. Talking to Angélica, Estrella confides her fears about both marriage and the man she is engaged to: "Augusto's character, Cousin, is not likely to bring happiness to a woman who has been educated with some idea of independence, and, as you know, my dear father reared me just that way. Augusto calls dignity in a man what I call authority, and it displeases him to discover these beliefs in me that he considers inappropriate for a woman. And besides, it is not possible for anyone to convince me that God has excluded us from the pleasure of liberty. Nor can I resign myself, as most women do, to the role of martyr in my marriage."[25] Angélica prudently encourages her cousin to abandon these dangerous ideas and to get what she wants through persuasion, not rebellion.

In her revealing poem "Contestación," written in 1855, Luisa Pérez de Zambrana again suggests her ambivalence about accepting women's secondary status and questioning that role. In response to a male friend who has encouraged her to pursue her interest in poetry and has advised her to expand her life experiences to improve her writing, she laments:

And do you ask me, respected friend,
That I devote myself to studying day and night,

That I open my mind, and elevate myself
on the beautiful wings of Poetry
to the ethereal region, that I greedily embrace
the time in which we live, that I tirelessly
ennoble my ardent fantasy
with sublime objects; that I refine my taste,
and I ply the immense seas,
and, opening my soul to great impressions,
boldly set foot in foreign lands?

The poet passionately acknowledges how much she longs for the opportunities men have, how she dreams of finding herself on a ship, a symbol of freedom for people who live on an island like Cuba:

Oh, and if you only knew how my soul, burning
with throbbing emotion takes delights in the
intoxication and seduction
of seeing the turgid sails open,
the linen float, the anchor rise,
the creaking of the keel and like the swift wind
fly through the blue immensity . . .! Oh, Lord
Tear, tear for the mercy of the soul
that impossible and mad illusion.

Hasn't her friend realized that, as a young woman, and an orphan, too, she is free to do no such thing? Comparing women's fate to that of the slave, a provocative simile in Cuba's plantation society, Pérez de Zambrana's words are filled with anger and resignation:

I inspire compassion in you, well, then, you know,
Nothing I can be, I am a slave
Woman that I am, with neck bowed
To the strong yoke that unjustly deprives us
Of the delicious freedom that men
Happily and endlessly enjoy.
How many times I cried bitterly
Over this terrible custom!
My good friend,
You already know how much I have against me,
and how I fight to conquer! Oh, do not be

offended
If I do not yield to your affectionate invitation
Since you know that in this unjust world
as young, female, and orphan I am powerless.[26]

Similar dissatisfaction with women's subjugation, and far less ambivalence, can be found in Gertrudis Gómez de Avellaneda, one of the more daring and original romantic writers of the Spanish-speaking world. In a series of articles she wrote for a Cuban newspaper, Gómez de Avellaneda analyzes the female condition and poses the question of "whether the Universal Father, while enriching [women] with the heart's treasures, deprived them, however, of the great faculties of intellect and character."[27] Looking for answers, Gómez de Avellaneda searched for women role models from the past who could demonstrate female valor, a sign, as she saw it, of moral strength. She diligently lists every example of a woman—whether from the pages of the Bible or from historical accounts—who performed brave or heroic acts. She found quite a few, even if the edifying nature of these deeds escapes the contemporary reader. There was Deborah, who declared war on the Canaanites; Jahel, who hammered Sisara to death; Judith, who cut off Holofernes's head and served it on a silver tray; the women of Sparta, who heroically fought Pirro; Tebas's daughters, who were willing to sacrifice themselves for their city; and Boadicea, who helped kill seventy thousand Romans to avenge her enslaved people. She lists Joan of Arc as well as Charlotte Corday, "who tainted her delicate hand with Marat's filthy blood."[28] She examines women who held positions of power, culminating with Queen Isabella of Spain, the definite proof of a woman's capability in Gómez de Avellaneda's eyes. She also studies female intellectual power, an area where she found scant evidence of activity, so had to content herself with a mention of Sappho's poems and little else.

Nonetheless, Gómez de Avellaneda deemed her findings proof of female worthiness. She concludes: "In nations where the woman is honored, in which her influence dominates society, there you will surely find civilization, progress, and public life. In countries where the woman is devalued, there is nothing that is great; servitude, barbarism, and moral ruin are the inevitable fate to which they are condemned."[29]

In her writing and in her life, Gómez de Avellaneda pointed the way to an alternative view of womanhood, but few could follow her. Unlike most of her female contemporaries, she was unapologetically ambitious. She was fully aware of her talent and expected society to take notice. When recognition came, it had a price not many women were willing to pay. "There's much man in this woman," says Bretón de los Herreros, a Spanish writer and admirer, summing up the general feeling that a woman of Gómez de Avellaneda's literary genius could not be a true woman. After her death, Cuban writer and leader of the independence movement, José Martí, wrote: "There was nothing feminine about Gertrudis Gómez de Avellaneda; everything about her was powerful and masculine; her body was tall and robust, and her poetry rough and forceful; there was no tender look in her eyes, but, instead, they would burn with authority: she was like a menacing cloud. There is a haughty, even fierce, man in the poetry of Avellaneda."[30]

In her novel *Dos mujeres* (*Two Women*) (1842), set and published in Spain, where the writer spent most of her adult life, Gómez de Avellaneda is brave enough to address the explosive subject of marriage and the devastating effect this institution could have on women. The novel tells the story of a young man in a quiet provincial town who, at his family's request, marries his pure, innocent cousin. Business obligations take him to Madrid, where a cosmopolitan, sophisticated woman seduces him. Although feeling tremendous guilt for betraying his wife, the man loves the other woman. The conflict comes to a conclusion when his lover, generously, commits suicide, freeing him from any commitment and allowing him to go back to his wife. He does so, but he cannot love her, and they both live miserably until the end of their lives.

In the story's epilogue, Gómez de Avellaneda argues that the indissolubility of marriage chains both men and women to an unhappy fate. But it is women, with a weaker standing in society, who will eventually suffer the consequences of a failed romance. Whether as the offended or the offending party, whether as a virtuous victim or a guilty seductress, women will be destroyed, since society has no compassion for either one.[31]

Dos mujeres was banned in Cuba for containing immoral doctrines. Considered even more dangerous was the content of the first abolitionist Cuban novel, *Sab*, which Gómez de Avellaneda wrote when she was only twenty-four. *Sab*, published in 1841, eleven years before Harriet Beecher Stowe's *Uncle Tom's Cabin*, shocked Cuban society not simply because it questions the morality of slavery but also because its main character, Sab, is an intelligent, dignified, manly slave who is passionately in love with Carlota, his white mistress. She is a more conventional character, a compendium of nineteenth-century female qualities who favors, instead, Enrique Otway, an Englishman settled in Cuba, who is not half as worthy as the slave. Although Carlota, as a proper Cuban lady, is innocently unaware of Sab's devotion, another white woman,

Teresa, is so deeply moved by the slave's character that she wants to tie her fate to his: "I am the woman who entrusts yourself to you. Allow me, then, to follow you to remote climes, to the heart of the wilderness. I will be your friend, your companion, your sister!"[32] Teresa's words sent tremors through Cuban society.

The novel does more than expose the injustice of the slave system, however. It is a study of the contrasts between modern commercial values, as embodied in Enrique's materialistic, calculating philosophy, and traditional Cuban values, as represented by Sab's spirituality and generosity. Enrique and his masculine world triumph in this story, while Sab, Carlota, Teresa, and, by extension, Cuba lose out. But Gómez de Avellaneda's critique of slavery was what scandalized her society. "It is truly a terrible life," says Sab, referring to the life of a slave:

> Under this fiery sky the nearly naked slave works all morning without rest, and at the terrible hour of midday, panting, crushed under the weight of the wood and the sugarcane he bears on his shoulders, scorched by the rays of the sun that burn his skin, the unhappy soul at last gets a taste of all the pleasures which life holds for him: two hours of sleep and a frugal meal. When night comes with its breezes and shadows to console the scorched land and all nature rests, the slave with his sweat and tears waters the place where neither the night has shadows nor the breeze, freshness, because there the heat of firewood has replaced that of the sun and the unhappy black walks endlessly around either the machine which extracts the cane's sweet juice or the cauldrons in which the fire's heat converts this juice into molasses; hour after hour he sees go by, and the sun's return finds him there still. Ah, yes! The sight of this degraded humanity, where men become mere brutes, is a cruel spectacle. These are men whose brows are seared with the mark of slavery just as their souls are branded with the desperation of hell.[33]

With *Sab*, Gómez de Avellaneda addressed the most highly charged, controversial topic of her time. The institution of slavery defined nineteenth-century Cuban society and thereby shaped women's lives. Slavery inevitably poisoned the environment in which women of the well-to-do-classes lived and made their indolent existence possible. Slavery assigned black women a subordinate economic, social, and sexual role while it permitted the leisurely, impractical education white women received. Speaking of how slavery poisoned the character of white Cuban women, Anselmo Suárez y Romero, author of the abolitionist novel *Francisco*, which he wrote in 1838 but was not published until 1889, states: "From the time she opened her eyes she began to give orders, and this custom of being obeyed destroyed the patience that she might have developed with a different kind of upbringing, a typical defect of the daughters of Cuba."[34]

While white women had little contact with the slaves working in the fields, they lived in close proximity to their domestic slaves. The black girl was the white girl's playmate when they were little, and her confidant in adolescence. Yet for all their closeness in these early years, their worlds could not have been farther apart. The former could expect her needs to be taken care of, to receive an education, to dress in fine clothes, to attend social gatherings, to meet friends, to marry, to nurture her children; the latter could take nothing for granted. In 1878, Camagüeyan writer Aurelia Castillo raised a red flag about the moral effect slavery had on white Cuban woman: "Even before she becomes accustomed to dozens of voices, her ears already know the words master and slave. When the children's games begin, her playmate is another little girl of the same age. But this girl is black, and this color draws a rigid line between them. The black girl finds herself suffering from all of the perverse impulses of the other, or maybe it is simply that fleeting malevolence that can be found in children, but she cannot retaliate. And the other knows, even in her innocence, her absolute power, and the former her absolute submission."[35] Dismissing claims of benevolence that slave owners often made, Aurelia Castillo asks "her sisters" to realize that neither sweetness nor compassion can compensate for all that was taken away from the slaves. Without home or family, without past or future, argues Castillo, the slave is deprived of an identity.

She ends her analysis with a warning to Cuban women that slavery's moral degradation affects not only the slaves but also the masters (or, in this case, the mistresses): "Think, dear ladies, that every chain has two ends, and when there is a servant at one end, there will be a master at the other, both bound and both miserable. Break forever this chain, generously redeem all of the beings who are under your rule, and from this time on, educate your daughters so that, without taking away their spirituality, they will be able to better respond to what daily life demands of them."

Castillo's words, like much of Cuba's antislavery literary tradition, make it clear that slavery was an obstacle to the normal development of a white Cuban woman's body and soul. For women to achieve true adulthood—social, moral, and political—the slave system had to be eradicated. Even women who defended the status quo could not deny the negative impact slavery had on marriage relations. A common condition of the affluent Cuban home was the master's *concubinato* (concubinage) with his young slaves. From the mistress's point of view, Castillo complained, the voluptuous, uninhibited female slave threatened domestic peace. She was blamed for the head of the family's or, in some cases, the young master's sexual affairs, when in reality she often became their victim as soon as she reached puberty.[36]

In Félix Tanco's *Petronila and Rosalía*, written in 1838 but not published until 1925 because of its explosive social critique, two generations of female slaves are destroyed when they become the object of their masters' sexual advances. Petronila, the mother, lives with relative ease as the domestic slave of a rich Havana family. When her mistress discovers that Petronila is pregnant, the young slave, to her horror, is banned permanently to the family plantation as punishment for her sin. "I cannot allow scandals of such a kind in my home," her mistress complains.[37] The father of Petronila's baby turns out to be the master, but, predictably, he will do nothing to protect her.

Rosalía, the daughter of this union, spends her early years at the plantation with her mother until the mistress, taking a fancy to her, decides to bring her to their home in Havana. As soon as the girl reaches adolescence, the cycle is repeated, this time, the offender being the young master. Rosalía, too, is sent away, as soon as her pregnancy is discovered. When the mistress confronts her son, he laughingly discards the subject as unimportant: "But Mamita, these are things men do, we can't avoid it."[38] An interesting and unusual aspect of this story is that, at first, the white master, with a doctor's collaboration, tries but fails to abort Petronila's pregnancy. The mistress also tries it with Rosalía, but again to no avail. According to the Spanish law, the child of a free man and a slave was born free, but only if the father acknowledged his paternity. Often, as is the case in this story, he would not, and the offending woman would be sent away or sold.

The subject of the paterfamilias's sexual affair with a slave, an action replicated by his son, is a nearly constant theme in nineteenth-century Cuban literature. Men did not risk their good standing in society for such trifles as fathering an illegitimate child with a slave. Their friends and associates looked the other way. Their wives, apart from private displays of anger, had little recourse in a society where divorce was not an option and men had unquestioned authority over women's lives.

But it would be a mistake to assume that women's vulnerable position made it impossible for them to have a happy family life. Sherry Johnson argues that the focus on gender relations within the context of sexual liaisons in much of nineteenth-century Cuban literature distorts the reality of black and white

women's lives, most of whom, including many slaves, were in long-lasting rela-
tionships.[39] In fact, throughout the century, marital relations became less formal and more affectionate, partly as a result of the influence of romanticism.
Nevertheless, tradition continued to mold the behavior of Cuban husbands
and wives. Their roles and spheres were well defined. The father controlled the
family's finances and made the most important decisions; the mother instilled
religious values in her children and administered the home. The father was
feared and respected; the mother tended to forge strong emotional ties with
her sons and daughters.

In *Cecilia Valdés*, Villaverde provides an illuminating example of family
dynamics. The wife and children of a powerful slave trader are having lunch at
home. For the hour the father is present, the family eats in a silence that is
broken only by the sound of clattering silver. After having coffee, he moves to
the smoking room, leaving his family on its own. "The disappearance of the
father figure alone meant a sudden and complete change not only in the spirit
and conduct of the family but also in the mother. The children's hearts were
lightened, it would seem, from an oppressive weight, and everyone's tongues
were freed as though in chorus."[40]

The same dynamic is replicated in *Sofía*, a novel set in the 1880s. When the
head of the household, "that serious and morose man[,] left the table, everyone eating would feel relieved, even the servants who waited on them; and a
general lighthearted feeling would take over."[41] In both cases, the father is the
authority figure in the family before whom confidences cannot be exchanged,
true feelings displayed, or anecdotes recounted. This is hardly unusual in a
patriarchal society, yet in Cuba there was an additional element that made the
father an outsider. In many families, as in the two just mentioned, the father
was a Spaniard while the mother and children were Cuban. The mounting
political tension between the metropolis and the colony found a parallel within
the Cuban family.

Scholars of nationalism point out that women have commonly been asked
to mark the boundaries of national groups by limiting their marriage relations
to members of their own group, thereby playing a role in the creation of a
nationalist identity.[42] This was not the case in nineteenth-century Cuba, if we
consider how widespread intermarriage was between those born in Spain and
those born on the island. The census of 1862 records the disproportionate
number of white males between ages sixteen and sixty—300,926—compared
with white women of the same ages— 175,995—because of immigration.[43]
The characteristic immigrant to the island was a single Spanish man whose

goal was to marry a Cuban woman once he established himself in the new environment. If he succeeded, his origin inevitably made him and his wife view Spain's role in Cuba in different lights. Mothers had a complex role to fulfill: they were mediators between their husband and children in matters relating to discipline and behavior; they mediated, too, the political disputes between father and children that inevitably occurred in those homes where the head of the household came from the other side of the ocean.

But Cuban mothers did more than simply mediate. Their position as cultural insiders gave them a degree of power their Spanish husbands lacked, a power that helped them enter the realm of politics. In families where the father was a foreigner, it was the mother who transmitted her love of her country and knowledge of the island's nature, folk tales, legends, music, and culture to the next generation. Thus she played a key role in the development of a Cuban consciousness.[44] According to Victoria Caturla: "When it comes to the formation of a national identity in colonial society, mothers deserve as much credit as educators and philosophers. Dedicated heart and soul to the upbringing of their children, Creole mothers were constantly fostering in them a love of all things local, and, as true queens of the home, they surrounded themselves with the new customs that gradually breached the traditional ties to the metropolis. The Spaniards themselves recognized this when they said that they could do whatever they wanted in Cuba, except have Spanish children."[45]

Nineteenth-century women of the Cuban bourgeoisie lived an existence that was both pampered and confining. Their privileged position allowed them to relegate many of the household duties to slaves, while their lives were limited by strict social norms and lack of education. Throughout the century, however, Cuban society became increasingly exposed to and influenced by social, political, and cultural forces that undermined tradition. A gradual expansion of educational opportunities helped women begin to articulate their own views of the world and to question the state of their society. Their strong attachment to the land where they were born, whether that attachment was shared with their husbands, informed the women's anticolonial stand. While lacking political power, their position as cultural insiders gave women an influential role in shaping the political climate of their homes and communities.

Rather than the picture of a doll drawn by some foreigners, a more accurate portrait of Cuban women might have been captured by a Spanish writer who noticed with apprehension that the island's women had "an initiative and strength unknown in women from other regions, and a spirit of independence not proper, or common, fortunately, among the fair sex."[46] The spirit of rebellion against the metropolis's abuse resonated with Cuban women. In some cases, rebellion would be born with their help. Women closely connected with slaveholding and large business interests maintained their loyalty to the status quo, just as their male relatives did. Yet thousands of women from the comfortable classes, including many who owned domestic slaves, contributed in various ways to the insurgency. This nationalist sentiment gave them the strength to get out of their hammocks.

2

▲▼▲▼▲

The Whip

Black Women in a Slave Society

African slaves had been brought to Cuba since the early years of the Spanish Conquest. They were employed doing domestic chores or working as field hands on tobacco and sugar plantations. In urban areas, slaves often engaged in trades considered too lowly for Spaniards. They were the tailors, the bakers, the musicians and construction workers. By the late 1790s, about 100,000 slaves, a relatively small number, lived on the island. Although it was not benign, slavery in this early period lacked the brutality that would characterize the institution in the 1800s.

The 1791 revolution in St. Domingue made Cuba the world's number-one producer of sugar, and the growing demand for this product could be met only with a larger labor force. Between 1790 and the 1860s, therefore, Cuba received some half million African slaves, whose presence would forever transform the island's culture and society. The newcomers were not spread evenly throughout Cuba, but were concentrated in the western and central provinces, where the big sugar plantations flourished.

Camagüey, on the other hand, continued to have cattle as its main source of income, which made heavy investment in slaves unprofitable. Slavery was also a bad financial option in Oriente, where lack of capital to invest in technological innovations, such as the steam engine, and heavy taxes on exports made it difficult for the eastern elite to compete with the western sugar planters. Consequently, Oriente became home to the largest population of freed slaves, many of them making their living as small farmers or craftspeople.

Most slaves were destined for the rich plantations of Matanzas and Havana. With productivity and profits in mind, the plantation owners in the first decades of the nineteenth century were strictly interested in male slaves, who were considered stronger. As a result, in the early 1800s, more than 88 percent of the slave population was male.[1] Despite government attempts to encourage the purchase of women, and thereby facilitate natural reproduction among the enslaved population, sex ratios remained out of balance until the dangers of the slave trade, increasingly under international attack, forced the big planters to realize that raising slaves could be cheaper and safer than buying them.

In 1815, the Congress of Vienna publicly condemned the slave trade as inconsistent with the values of the civilized world. Two years later, Spain and Great Britain signed an agreement outlawing the slave trade, but that did not bring it to an end. *Cecilia Valdés* offers an example of how slave traders circumvented the law. Once a slave ship arrived at the port of Havana, the African men and women were given fresh new clothes to make them pass as slaves coming from Puerto Rico.[2] Yet, though it survived, the business of human trafficking became riskier, and purchasing slaves, more expensive. The need for women then became apparent, and the number of female slaves increased considerably by the mid-1800s.

Most African slaves in Cuba were purchased to work in the large cane fields belonging to the sugar mills. They came from various parts of western Africa, their owners often listing their nationality, or what they thought was their nationality, next to their name when they registered them: Lucumí, Ganga, Congo, Carabalí, Arara, Macua, Bibi, Suama, Briche. Traditionally the typical slave dwelling on a plantation was the *bohío*, a hut surrounded by a small field where a family could grow vegetables and raise chickens. In the 1840s, the plantation owners began to favor the barracoons, rectangular structures with a dirt floor, each consisting of several crowded rooms. Hundreds of slaves were locked in at night in these compounds allowing the master greater control over them. Slaves were let out before the sun was up to start working. According to the Reglamento de Esclavos (Slaves' Ruler) issued by the Spanish government in 1842, during the *zafra*, the collecting season, which lasted from December until May or June, slaves were to work between ten and twelve hours a day. They were to be allowed a two-hour rest during the day and six hours of sleep at night. During the noncollecting season, the Reglamento indicated that the slave should work nine or ten hours a day.[3] But in reality, during the harvest slaves worked sixteen to nineteen hours a day, no matter the weather conditions.

Female slaves worked side by side with the men and were expected to perform similar tasks. "There seemed to be little or no difference in the amount of work expected from the women or the men and, indeed, at first sight, it was not easy to discover any difference of sex," wrote New York *Herald* correspondent James O'Kelly. In her study of the slave family, Cuban historian María del Carmen Barcia argues that the slave owners, concerned as they were with increasing the numbers of slave children, as a way to expand their property, were careful not to overwork pregnant women, who were allowed shorter workdays.[4] Birth rates on the plantation, however, were unusually low and infant mortality was rampant. Women often miscarried or lost their babies within the first couple of weeks of delivery. The hardships of motherhood under the slave system led slave women to abort their pregnancies at times. Among the potions they used, the papaya fruit and leaves seem to have been particularly effective.[5] When a pregnancy was carried to full term and the baby survived, the mother was given a few weeks to recover, before being put to work again. Her baby was then left at the infirmary with an older black woman, who was in charge of raising the slave children until they reached the age of seven. According to article no. 8 of the Reglamento de Esclavos: "Black newborn babies or infants whose mothers go to work will be fed with light food, soups, corn flour gruel, milk, until they are weaned."[6] Not until the 1860s, only two decades before slavery was abolished, was any thought given to the need to improve the treatment of pregnant and nursing women by providing them more time to recover and to spend with their babies.[7]

Masters made deliberate attempts to increase their property by selecting strong, healthy men and women and forcing them to mate and breed: "After they were together in a separate room in the barracoon, they were obliged to have sex, and the woman had to bear good babies every year," reminisced a former slave. "I tell you it was like breeding animals. Well, if the woman didn't bear the way they liked, they separated them and put her out in the field again to work."[8]

Most often, it was the slaves themselves who chose to live with a mate, and masters, aware that married slaves would be less likely to run away and be troublesome, promoted the institution of marriage among them. The Reglamento of 1842 encouraged slave owners to provide separate rooms for married couples, as if the barracoon were a hotel with plenty of space. Also contemplated was the need to keep families together. If a slave woman married a slave from a different plantation, the husband's owner was responsible for buying her; if he refused to do so, the wife's owner should buy the husband; and if neither owner was interested, a third party should buy the married couple; the purchase should also include the female slave's children under age three. Since no real attempt was made to enforce this ruling, this legislation was merely a way to assuage the authorities' conscience. In fact, slave owners showed little concern about separating married couples, or slave mothers and their babies, as shown in the many ads that appeared in newspapers: "A black woman for sale with baby or without."[9]

The disregard for ties between mother and child, as well as for the bond between husbands and wives, along with the immense difficulties slaves faced when trying to maintain a sense of family have led some historians to question the survival of the institution of family among slaves. Clearly, the slave family could not conform to the standards and expectations of the middle class.[10] However, the evident distress that slaves endured when separated from their loved ones proves that, despite difficulties, slaves deeply valued their blood connections. Slave women made efforts to attend to their family's domestic needs—no easy task. A former slave explained: "In the center of the barracoons, the women washed their husbands' clothes, their children's and their own. They washed in washtubs. Washtubs during slavery weren't like today. Those then were more rustic. And you had to take them to the river so they would swell up to hold water because they were made of codfish boxes."[11]

Cuban writer and plantation owner Anselmo Suárez y Romero wrote of the slave women:

> One can say that these black women do not rest, not even on Sundays or holidays; these women seem to be made of steel. They sleep no more than five hours during the grinding process, and then they do housework, even the young girl, who, sighing, rises before daybreak, has to do with only a short noontime break, the time when they come home to eat. They cut sugarcane in the hot sun, a furnace in the tropics, and on top of all this, if there is a downpour, they must endure the water, and in winter, the cold, which in the fields is more piercing, chilling the African to the bone, and then on Sundays and holidays, they must breast-feed their child, wash and mend the clothes, cook—I don't know, I don't know how they can withstand so much![12]

It seems reasonable to assume that the slaves' strength had much to do with their love for and commitment to their families. A revealing aspect of the role women played in keeping the slave family united is to be found in the legal actions they brought against masters. Digna Castañeda shows how it was generally slave women who complained to the *síndico*, the government's appointed representative of the slaves, about the violation of their relatives' rights. They denounced the selling of infants—their children or grandchildren—who were theoretically protected by the 1842 Reglamento de Esclavos, and asked that children be allowed to remain with their mothers until they were three years old. They denounced masters who violated the *coartación*, the slaves' right to buy their freedom. And they complained when their sons, daughters, or husbands who were free were sold back into slavery. Although masters found it easy to deny these accusations, the legal action slave women took under the most difficult circumstances suggests, as Castañeda points out, that they were willing to use every possible means to keep their families together.[13]

Slaves also developed a sense of friendship and community with each other. In addition to having nights to themselves, they were able to avoid the control of white society on Sundays and other holidays. During this time, they played, made friends, met lovers, and worked on their *conucos*, small pieces of land where they were allowed to raise squash, beans, corn, and other vegetables as well as small animals, such as chicken or pigs. For the women, holidays were a time to take care of their families. They also enjoyed taking care of themselves: "Women combed their hair in curls in little rows. Their heads looked like Castilian melons. They liked that busy work of combing their hair one way one day and another way the next. One day with rows, another with curls, another, conked."[14]

On holidays, slaves also tried to re-create the cultural practices that had helped them (or their ancestors) make sense of the world before their enslavement. Owners allowed their slaves to enjoy music and dancing at the end of the week, as long as they stayed within the limits of their property. Music, dancing, religious practices, and games permitted the slaves to maintain their sanity and identity.

Magic potions and other forms of the supernatural gave slaves a sense of power, elevating them to a sphere beyond the white master's control. A witch —male or female—was one of the most useful members of the group, as she or he could cure disease, fend off enemies, reverse curses, and help out with love troubles. "If a man went to a witch to ask for help getting a woman, the witch sent him to get some of the woman's tobacco if she smoked. You ground up the tobacco and a bottle fly, those green, stinging ones, enough to make a powder, which you gave to the woman in water. This is how the woman was seduced."[15]

Older black women often took the position of spiritual leader, a natural role for them. Their jobs on the plantation as cooks, midwives, and nurses gave them unquestionable authority over the healing or harming power of food, herbs, and plants. It also gave them authority as doctors. Taking care of the sick at the infirmary kept older women busy all year long. Smallpox, dysentery, and yellow fever regularly hit the plantations, where unhygienic conditions turned the barracoons into cesspools for the spread of contagion. A limited diet of salted meat, cod, plantains, rice, corn flour, and sugar weakened slaves, as did the grueling work schedule they were forced to endure.

Long workdays, however, were nothing compared with the brutal punishments that masters and overseers imposed on slaves who did not submit to their authority. These remnants of a medieval world had a surprisingly sadistic quality. Whipping was usually done with the slave on the ground in a prone position, called, for this reason, *el bocabajo*, or facedown. If the offending slave happened to be a pregnant woman, a hole was excavated in which to fit her belly and avoid damaging the "merchandise."[16] Fernando Ortiz writes: "No old Cuban, or one who had a Creole mother who told him childhood stories of slavery, can ever forget the wailing of whipped slaves, the writhing of muscles when the whip cracked, the blood oozing from the broken skin, and the sorrowful begging for mercy, incessantly, to the rhythm of the whip."[17]

Stocks were common—in their mildest version, trapping both feet, at their worst, also the head. Shackles, clubs, and chains were also used to keep the slaves in line. Although in 1842 the Reglamento de Esclavos aimed to reduce the severity of physical punishment, the guidelines were never enforced. La Escalera, a slave conspiracy discovered in 1844, gave plantation owners the excuse they needed to maintain their brutally repressive system. They pressured the government to leave disciplining of slaves up to "the prudent discretion of the masters."[18]

The most prosperous sugar plantations housed three hundred or four hundred slaves. Only the continuous enforcement of discipline could keep this large labor force under control. As Isabel, a young character in *Cecilia Valdés* realizes, in the Cuban sugar mill "reigned a permanent state of war, a bloody, cruel, implacable war, black against white, the master against the slave." It is important, however, Barcia points out, to realize the complexity and variety of the slave experience. Not all slaves were submitted to physical punishment and, when they were, the master's goal, in most cases, was to teach them a lesson, not to cripple and render them useless.[19]

When life became unbearable for the slave, in addition to suicide, a common occurrence on Cuban plantations, he or she could try to run away. Newspaper ads regularly listed descriptions of fugitives: "Black Rosario, Creole, known as La Conga, has disappeared from her master's house, Crespo St., number 68, 13 years of age, tall, with large eyes, a thick lower lip, dressed in purple calico; anyone hiding her will be held liable for damages." And: "Black Teresa, Congolese, about 18 to 20 years of age, average height and with a scar on her cheek, had shackles on one foot with a dangling thin chain when she left her master's house; she was wearing a checked blue tunic, a shawl, and a scarf around her head. Anyone who has information about her will be rewarded with an ounce of gold and anyone hiding her will be held accountable. Galiano num. 35."[20]

Warnings against helping runaway slaves were mostly aimed at free blacks. As Pedro Deschamps Chapeaux has showed, one of the most significant ways in which Cubans of African descent challenged the system was to hide fugitive slaves. Free blacks living on the outskirts of the city were particularly well positioned to do this.[21] But masters used every power they had to get their property back. The Countess of Merlín recalled: "When a slave runs away, the foreman takes a dog to the fugitive's hut and has him sniff the Negro's clothes. Sometimes a fight ensues between the Negro and the dog, but the latter always has the advantage, and even if it's wounded will not release its prey. With admirable skill, it lightly jumps at its enemy, trying to grab his ears, and once it achieves this, it digs in its teeth so deeply that the Negro doubles up in pain and surrenders to his opponent, who is then happy to drag him up and lead him to where his companions are."[22]

For the fugitive slave, freedom could be found only by hiding in the most inaccessible, thickly wooded forests. There, *cimarrones*, as runaway slaves were called, created their own communities, or *palenques*. Successful *palenques*, those that had a stable and relatively long life, often included women and children.

Nineteenth-century Cuban literature has brutally vivid descriptions of the violence used against runaway slaves, but nothing can compare to Pedro José Morillas's "El ranchador" ["The Small Farmer"] (1846), a short story about a *guajiro*, a white peasant who, having lost his children in an attack by *cimarrones*, has devoted his life to killing runaway slaves. The *guajiro* describes to the story's narrator what happened after he located a *palenque* with the help of hounds and a convict: "I went along blind with rage while my companion laughed. At the top we found a clearing where some banana trees, yams, and other edible crops had been planted. There were ten robust Negroes, almost totally naked, or barely covered with filthy rags, and they were armed; some had shoes hardened in the fire, others had machetes, and they were trying to fend off the dogs while the majority of the group fled down the rougher side of the hill with their women, their children, and some of their pitiful household items."[23] A killing scene follows, including details of how the *cimarrones* met their death, some by the white men's machetes, some by musket fire, some devoured by the dogs. After the *guajiro's* partner collects the dead men's right ears, the credential required to receive a reward, they inspect the *cimarrones'* homes, finding almost nothing other than religious idols and objects, which the white men hurry to destroy as African superstition. The story ends with another encounter between the hunters and the black men, but this time the persecution is witnessed by the narrator: "Climbing laboriously up those rough paths, I finally reached the top, from which point I was able to make out, at the bottom of the ravine, two dogs tearing apart a wounded Negro with their fangs, so ferociously that he was unable to escape or defend himself, and three other unfortunates lying dead in a pool of their own steaming blood. The wounded Negro saw me and begged for my protection, but the dogs would not obey me or let me approach." The man dies, and the narrator leaves, cursing his country's "odious fate."[24]

This story reveals the difficulties that runaway slaves met when they attempted to survive in the forest, but it also suggests that some *palenques* had stability enough to include women and children. The fact that the runaway men were willing to die to protect their families points to the strong ties of affection that would have existed among members of such communities.

Urban slaves lived an easier and freer life than did plantation slaves. Although their condition as domestic servants placed them under the master's constant surveillance, town slaves generally performed lighter work, ate better food, dressed better, and lived in a less-repressive atmosphere than did their country counterparts. In urban centers, slave families often achieved a considerable degree of autonomy. In 1861, 70 percent of all slave families in Havana lived in a home separate from their masters'. Marriage between slaves and free blacks was not uncommon, and these mixed couples frequently lived by themselves.[25] Urban slaves also enjoyed more opportunities to gain their freedom. According to Spanish law, slaves had the right to buy their freedom if they could repay their master for their price or the average price slaves fetched at a given time. Slaves also had the right to change masters if they could find a new one willing to buy them. Despite the *conucos*, slaves living in the country had few opportunities to raise the funds required to buy their freedom. Slave women with a particular skill—cooking, ironing, sewing, and the like—were at times rented out and might be given a small compensation. And a midwife's skills were especially valued. In general, however, rural slaves' possibilities for saving money were limited. Nor did they have many chances to meet new masters interested in purchasing a slave who was particularly unhappy with his or her situation.

City slaves, on the other hand, ran errands for their masters and mistresses, entered stores, socialized with free blacks, interacted with whites on the streets, and had opportunities to meet a wide variety of people, who, potentially, could help them improve their status. In some cases, black women obtained their freedom as a result of their sexual interaction with white men.

The city's looser racial lines, however, did not always translate into advantages for the slave. Doting white men's attentions often came up disappointingly short of the black women's expectations. One popular form of entertainment for affluent young white man was socializing and flirting with black women at dances attended by both these groups. The women's vulnerable position made them prey to unscrupulous young men.

In one passage of the novel *Sofía*, a female slave is trying to convince her friend Sofía to attend one of these parties. When Sofía questions the morality of such events, her friend argues that much happiness comes out of them and tells the story of another slave, María Roca. At one of those parties, her young white admirer, Ricardo Bonanza, married her and freed her. A confused and doubtful Sofía asks how they could be married. Her friend replies: "It was a secret wedding. One of the young men there, with the priest's permission, brought the robes and all, and using the table in the room as an altar, married them just as if he'd been a minister of the Lord. We were all witnesses. And before reaching the altar, what do you think Ricardo gave María Roca? No less than her freedom papers, girl, which he'd been carrying around in his pocket for days without her knowing! So you see what comes of those sinful meetings."[26] Sofía is quite impressed by María Roca's good fortune, "without imagining for a second that all that business of the wedding could be a vulgar scheme, what the modern youth called a *taquería* and which, at the most, cost the young spendthrift of the wealthy Bonanza family a couple of thousand duros."[27]

Most urban slaves were Creoles, born in Cuba, as opposed to the predominantly African plantation slaves. They were familiar with the language and customs and could navigate easily through the island's society. Before emancipation, a long and gradual process in Cuba, which began in the 1860s and ended in the 1880s, slaves who gained their freedom entered the growing population of free blacks who made a living as craftspeople, artisans, or skilled workers. The men became tailors, carpenters, and musicians; the women worked as bakers, cooks, midwives, and innkeepers. The city's racial intermingling exposed the various groups to each other's traditions and values and allowed a cultural—and a biological—synthesis. Blacks and whites became inseparable ingredients of nineteenth-century Cuban culture to such a degree that, in the popular imagination, by the late 1800s, the new sense of national identity was closely associated with the process of racial integration.

Racial interaction, however, did not always result in an expansion of rights for the black population. In fact, because of the frequent amalgamation, in the mid-1800s, laws were passed to prevent intermarriage and to limit free blacks' role in society. Blacks were excluded from hotels, theaters, and other public spaces. When those laws instituted in the 1860s began to relax in the 1880s and the 1890s, legal unions between blacks and whites continued to be rare.[28]

But even if not socially acceptable, among the well-to-do classes, the white man–black woman interaction was common at all social levels. For a black woman there was always the hope that her affair with a white man would elevate her social status. "In the shadow of the white man," writes Villaverde in *Cecilia Valdés*, "no matter how illicit her union, Cecilia hoped and believed she would always move up, that she would be able to escape her humble origins, or if not she, at least her children would. Married to a mulatto, she would descend in her own eyes and those of her peers, since such are the aberrations of a society such as the Cuban one."[29]

The term *saltoatrás*, or throwback, was applied to a child darker than his or her mother; this description graphically captured the value that associated whitening with improvement. For a free *mulata*, like the character Cecilia embodies, having children with a black man would pull her many steps down the social ladder that her family had been painstakingly ascending for several generations.

If not marriage, the young black woman could at least hope for presents, social connections, or an improvement of her living conditions. How often that turned out to be the case is hard to say, but it is likely that free black women, like female slaves, became the prey of the *señoritos'* fancy.

In Francisco Calcagno's novel *Romualdo*, a priest is scandalized to hear an old black woman, who is free, admit nonchalantly that various men—black and white—fathered her children: "My husband? We don't use one." When the priest looks at her reprovingly, she responds proudly: "And is it our fault?" The priest, sanctimoniously, has to agree: "It is true, how can we blame you poor unfortunate ones? Hasn't society abandoned you? Why do you have to account for your wrongdoings? Who teaches you to distinguish right from wrong? What schools are open to you? You are but pitiful instruments of pleasure that men break and stomp on after using, your virtue is reduced to your discretion; it is already quite virtuous of you not to make a fuss."[30]

Racial interaction was particularly intense among the lower and lower-middle classes. Throughout the second half of the nineteenth century, thousands of poor Spanish men arrived in Cuba looking for economic opportunities. The immigrants, mostly peasants from impoverished Spanish regions such as Galicia and the Canary Islands, soon began to compete with the free black men for jobs and women. As Verena Martínez-Alier (Stolcke) has pointed out, the Catholic Church asked repeatedly that any restrictions on interracial marriage be eliminated as the only way to prevent the sinful and popular practice of concubinage.[31] In 1867, the bishop of Havana complained: "Everywhere adultery and concubinage persist, largely between white men and mulatto women, producing an excessive number of natural offspring which with the exception of a few who are recognized by their progenitors it can be said have neither family nor society, for this consists of no more than a mother."[32] It is not surprising, then, that the children of this racially mixed group would identify not with their father's national background—especially when the father failed to act as one—but with their mother's Creole roots.

For all its conflicted views about slavery, the challenge to the Spanish authorities came to be associated with the abolitionist sentiment. For black women, free or slave, maintaining the colonial status quo meant the survival of an oppressive, unjust system that considered them disposable. On the other hand, the idea of Cuba Libre conjured up a powerful vision of freedom and justice for them and their children.

From the 1790s through the mid-1860s, almost half a million Africans were brought to Cuba as slaves. Most of them were taken to the big plantations of the central and western provinces, where they endured painful working and living conditions. Women were submitted to the same hardships as the men, making motherhood a particularly difficult ordeal. The slaves tried to maintain their sense of identity in various ways: they fought to keep their families together; re-created African cultural practices; and ran away. City slaves lived in a freer, more comfortable environment, though their frequent interaction with the white society, characterized as it was by an unequal power relation, placed them in a permanently tenuous position. For both the enslaved population and the emancipated slave, the fight against Spain offered a chance to find a place in Cuban society.

3

▲▼▲▼▲

Hair and Prayer

Early Signs of Unrest

Signs of Cuban women's interest in politics were already visible in the early 1800s. Spaniards noticed the unusual interest that Cuban women had in current events and were particularly scandalized at their identification with the French Revolution. Indeed, France's political challenge to the Old Regime, which the Revolution initiated and to which Napoleon Bonaparte gave a final blow, supplied the men and women of Cuba's educated classes with an endless source of inspiration. Even French fashion took on a political meaning.

One of Bonaparte's measures to modernize the French army was to put an end to wigs and long hair among its officers. When, in 1807, Napoleon invaded Spain and forced the Spanish king and his heir into exile, Cuba's authorities, afraid that the colonies would use this opportunity to air their own grievances, quickly passed repressive laws to curtail potential disturbances on the island. To protest these measures and to show their support for the spirit of reform France symbolized, Cuban women cut their hair, braids and curls. This new fashion contrasted with the more traditional styles Spanish women continued to display and was ridiculed in the conservative media. *Pelonas*, or baldies, was the nickname progovernment forces gave to women who cut their hair. Creole society, however, came to the defense of the *pelonas* and attacked the silly hairstyles of the *godas*, or Spanish women, saying it made them look like vermin.[1]

A letter to the editor in the newspaper *Aviso de la Habana* argued that women needed to cut their hair to simplify the cumbersome styles that bound them. By abandoning the fashion of elaborate curls and fake braids, by discarding gauze, coifs, combs, sequins, and other rubbish, Cuban women were moving with the times.[2] Long or short, up or down, hairstyle would be a recurrent tool that Cuban women used as a symbolic marker of national difference, to make political statements throughout this contentious century.

As old loyalties to Spain began to fade, advocates for reform increasingly looked not only to France but also to a source of inspiration closer to home. During the first half of the nineteenth century, Cubans who longed for the liberalization of their economy and society, but were also interested in maintaining the institution of slavery, naturally gravitated to the American model. Beginning in 1810, and almost every decade until the 1860s, prominent Cuban leaders approached the U.S. government with requests to be admitted into the union. Cuban annexationists hailed the path Texas had taken—from Mexican territory, to independent nation, to state. After all, they argued, the island's chief trading partner was not Madrid but Washington. By 1850, annual trade with the United States was 7.5 million pesos, 10 percent higher than trade with Spain.[3]

But the appeal of the United States was not merely economic. Cuba's northern neighbor, with its commitment to progress, technology, and democracy, embodied the enlightened values that the Cuban middle classes admired. By joining the United States, annexationists pointed out, Cubans' economic and political freedom would be greatly expanded.[4]

As the island began to consider a future separate from Spain, the question of what it meant to be Cuban took on new significance. Cuban intellectuals, through their writing, participated in the attempt to define the island's identity. In novels, plays, short stories, and travelogues, they explored local traditions and folklore as they tried to give a distinct voice to their people. Joining this effort was the Countess of Merlín, a Cuban aristocrat and writer, who returned to the island in 1840 after many years abroad. Although not welcomed by her colleagues, who dismissed her as a foreigner and a woman, the countess's *Viaje a la Habana*, as Adriana Méndez Rodenas has pointed out, is a significant contribution to identifying Cuba's singularity.[5] The letters about her trip combine celebratory descriptions of the island's climate and vegetation—the types of fruits and trees that grew exuberantly, so different from the European ones—with references to food, dances, customs, traditions, and the human types characteristic of Cuban society. Despite her loyalty to the colonial power—she never questioned Spain's right to rule Cuba—the countess was highly critical of the metropolis, an obstacle to the island's modernization. She contrasted the intellectual pursuits and the love of progress she found among her compatriots to the ignorance and corruption of the priests and bureaucrats sent to the island by Spain. Admonishing Spain to stop exploiting Cuba's resources, she called for political reform and change.[6]

Those involved in the process of imagining the island not as a Spanish appendage but as having its own entity had to address one question: Who deserved to be considered Cuban? Creole society reasoned that *peninsulares* (Spaniards living in Cuba), with their explicit allegiance to Madrid, could not be counted as such. Neither could the island's population of African descent, which by mid-century, including both free blacks and slaves, had reached half a million, a third of the population. In fact, excluding blacks from the Cuban tapestry became a major concern for whites engaged in the national-identity debate. The Creole bourgeoisie during this period defined its Cuban identity in opposition to both what was Spanish and what was African, an impossible balancing act. Criticism of the incompetent colonial government was accompanied by a discussion of the need to "whiten" the island. Putting an end to the slave trade was viewed as a step in the right direction, but insufficient. The best solution, some argued, was to deport free blacks to Africa and gradually replace African labor with that of white immigrants.

The growth of the black population deeply worried Creole society. Those who owned slaves understood that their wealth was based on the continuing presence of a black population that they feared. But members of the educated classes, who no longer benefited as slaveholders, viewed the Africanization of the island as a major obstacle to their goal of modernization. Ideas about black inferiority merged with the belief that a racially heterogeneous population could not thrive. Cuban professionals and businessmen viewed themselves as "modern" men who favored new venues for industry, commerce, and technology. Slavery was not so much immoral as antiquated, they claimed, an obstacle to the development of a capitalist economy and a free republic.

Yet contemplating what would happen were slavery abolished gave many of these "modern" men tremors. How would the slaves behave if they were liberated? Images of revengeful blacks killing their former masters and raping their mistresses pervaded the consciousness of Cuba's white society, a fear the Spanish authorities used to discredit any challenge to the status quo.

In *Sab*, Sab, the slave, evokes the warning of an old Indian woman: "The earth which once was drenched in blood will be so again: the descendants of the oppressors will be themselves oppressed, and black men will be terrible avengers of those of copper color." Don Carlos, Sab's owner, angrily orders the slave to be silent, Gómez de Avellaneda explains, "for the Cubans, always in a state of alarm after the frightful and recent example of a neighboring island [Haiti], could never hear without fear any words in the mouth of a man of that unfortunate color which made patent the feeling of his abused rights and the possibility of recapturing them."[7]

Anxiety and fear, however, did not diminish the Creole bourgeoisie's discontent, particularly in the eastern provinces. Its preoccupation with the island's future was exemplified by the growth of "civic societies" that engaged in a cultural and political discourse. Many of these societies, composed largely of the well-to-do, had an annexationist bent. More significantly, the groups were hotbeds of national sentiments and ideals, laboratories where a sense of *cubanidad* was forged. Havana, Santiago, Puerto Príncipe, Trinidad, Bayamo, Holguín, and Manzanillo were among the towns that established cultural societies (*sociedades*). Together with Masonic lodges, another important venue for political discussion, the *sociedades* articulated the opposition to the Spanish government. Even though they excluded women, female complicity was required, since the conspirators often met and hid in private homes. Reason and passion mingled in these groups' discussions, as talks on the latest agricultural techniques were followed with fervent pronouncements about the need to fight for a newly sacred ideal: *la patria* (the fatherland).

As patriotic feelings among the Cuban population increased, so did tensions between colonial authorities and their subjects. By mid-century, the island's political temperature was reaching a boiling point. Joaquín and Josefa de Agüero's lives illustrate the dangerous turn events could take for those involved in antigovernment activity. The couple also exemplifies how, by the 1850s, privileged Cubans were willing to risk everything for the elusive ideal that *la patria* embodied.

Josefa de Agüero, born in 1818 in Camagüey, married her cousin Joaquín de Agüero when she was very young. He had a substantial fortune, as well as a reformer's spirit, which he attributed to his mother's influence. He used his money to found a rural school for the poor children of Guáimaro. In 1843, burdened by moral qualms, he emancipated his eight slaves. "What right does a man have to take another by force and sell him as if he were his property?" asked Joaquín.[8]

Such abolitionist positions challenged the status quo. After Spanish officials questioned Agüero about his political views, he and Josefa, feeling unsafe, briefly moved to New York. There they joined a growing community of Cuban exiles, many of whom favored annexation. Agüero became a convert to this cause.

Three months later, back in Cuba, the Agüeros continued to associate with other Cubans who aspired to bring the ideals of progress and enlightenment to the island. In an atmosphere of increasing political tension, Agüero took a leading role in the struggle against Spain. He was among the first to join the *sociedad* of Puerto Príncipe. He got hold of a manual printing press and leafleted the province with antigovernment propaganda.

In 1850, Narciso López, a Venezuelan veteran of the South American wars of independence, landed in Cárdenas with almost five hundred filibusters, most of them recruited in the United States. This was his second attempt to help Cubans free the island from Spain. López, funded by a group of American plantation owners, hoped to convince the Cuban population to join the United States once the colonial government was defeated. The military venture met with failure and López was executed. But his martyrdom gave new hope to the opposition forces and confirmed Agüero's conviction that Cubans were ready to break with Spain.[9]

In 1851, the colonial government of Puerto Príncipe, alarmed by the growing discontent, attempted to crush the insurgency and arrested a score of rebel leaders, all members of the Camagüey elite. Agüero and a few of his friends were able to escape to the mountains between Nuevitas and Las Tunas. From these mountains Agüero, under the mistaken assumption that others would follow, organized the first significant rebellion against the colonial power.[10]

Adolfo Pierra, a young Camagüeyan who joined Joaquín de Agüero's uprising, reminisced years later that the women rushed to help the rebels. Meeting in secret at Josefa Agüero's home, they made flags for the soldiers and bandages for the wounded men.[11] One of these women, Martina Pierra, who was Adolfo's sister and only sixteen years old, captured the excitement of these days in a sonnet she composed in Agüero's honor:

Of Liberty, sublime and glorious
receive the banner Camagüeyans;
with enthusiasm unfurl it proudly,
the happy moment has arrived.
Make it always flutter beautifully
in your firm and brave hands,
and the banner the tyrants taunt

destroy, with wondrous blow!
Brave men, fight, while to the heavens
we pray fervently
so that God will soon give us the happiness
to see our beautiful country free.
Fight, fight, that Victory merrily
shows you the temple of Glory.[12]

The people of Camagüey held their breath, waiting for events to unfold. Even if only a few of them were ready to join the rebellion, Joaquín de Agüero was one of their own, his values and ideals similar to theirs.

We know far less about Josefa de Agüero than about her husband. Her solidarity with his politics, however, is decidedly conveyed in a letter she wrote to him on June 13, 1851, as he hid in the mountains preparing for military action. Using passionate but formal language, she addresses her husband: "I keep asking the Almighty God to transmit to every Cuban's heart an ardent desire to free their country. With great love, I would hold you tightly and say: 'Til we sing victory on earth or we enjoy the glory of heaven! I hope that you send for me once you secure a position, so that I have the pleasure of making myself useful."[13] Her missive clearly conveys her patriotic feelings and commitment to the insurgency. She also expresses the hope that God will help a cause she considers sacred.

Unable to take an active role in politics or military action, Josefa de Agüero turned to prayer as a way to influence the outcome of events. Two weeks later, with Joaquín still hiding in the mountains, Josefa again expressed her faith in heaven's help, and reiterated her support of the rebellion:

> My love, my life: It has been two months since you parted from me against my will, and that saved you from being expatriated. Let us pray to God that this country to which you have consecrated your life and for which you have suffered so much ... will finally be reconquered. Oh my dear husband! I wish I had the joy to be there in this sublime moment! It would be such pleasure to shake hands with each of those leaders! I would embrace you so lovingly! But since my two children prevent me from being there, I send you and them prayers from my heart. My adored husband, true courage is always prudent: Do not take offense if I beg you that on all occasions (as I have always seen you do) use a prudent judgment. Good-bye my heart, my life, my sole and only love—J.[14]

Nineteenth-century Cuban women were devout Catholics. Catholic rituals punctuated and marked the passing of time. Attending church services and activities gave women a reason to leave their houses and interact with other women. A woman often respected a priest, especially her confessor, as much as she did her father or husband. But the piety of Cuban women, like many other fundamental beliefs, was shaken by the support the church gave the colonial government. The Catholic Church in Cuba was very much a Spanish institution. Many of the priests and nuns who directed parishes and schools had been sent to the island directly from Spain. Although not a unified force, as seen by the number of the clergy who dissented from the official position, church authorities tended to be closely allied with the slaveholding classes and to support the status quo. As nineteenth-century Cuban writer Francisco Calcagno notes in *Romualdo*, priests, in order to protect owners, commonly issued death certificates for slaves who had died under suspicious circumstances.[15] If a master's punishment killed a slave, the best way to silence questions about the use of excessive force was to have a priest's complicity in presenting the matter as a case of death by natural causes.

The church's loyalty to Spain left pious Cuban women in an unsettling position. The experience of Josefa Agüero is a good example of the breach the war created between women and the church. Hoping to assist her husband, she asked the women of Camagüey to order daily masses to pray for the triumph of the coup. She herself embroidered a revolutionary flag, which she displayed during the services. "I have organized several ladies so that every church holds a solemn mass to pray to the God of the armies to hand you the victory," she wrote to her husband. "Mine will be on the 4th and we will put the [flag?] behind a statue."[16]

Accounts differ as to what transpired next. The official army version is that one of Joaquín de Agüero's comrades betrayed his chief and turned him in to the authorities. But according to the most accepted version of events, Josefa confessed everything to her priest, trusting he would honor the sanctity of the confessional. He did not. Instead, he went straight to the Spanish authorities and warned them of the rebellion. Based on this information, many of the men involved in the revolutionary coup were imprisoned and some, including Joaquín de Agüero, were condemned to death. Whether this is an accurate description of events, the popular imagination assigned one role to Josefa, even if an unwilling one, and another to her priest. The resulting lesson to Cuban women was that the Catholic Church was not to be trusted.[17]

After Joaquín de Agüero's arrest, a group of Camagüeyan women went to

General Lemerey, the highest-ranking Spanish authority, to beg for mercy. They brought with them a portrait of Queen Isabella II, hoping to invoke her power to intercede.[18] In making their request, the women adopted an unusually visible public role, but one that was both politically safe—they showed their obedience to the colonial government by using the royal image—and within traditional feminine confines. After all, it was a woman's prerogative to intercede, just as the Virgin Mary had mediated with her son on behalf of sinners. Adolfo Pierra, one of the rebels captured with Agüero, remembered the concern the women showed for the prisoners: "The people of Puerto Príncipe took an immense interest in our fate, especially the ladies and young women of the leading families, who often came to see us through the bars of the jail during visiting hours."[19]

Despite their support, Joaquín de Agüero and three of his comrades were executed. After Agüero's death, Josefa, his widow, went out of her mind for several days. One witness wrote: "Pepilla [Josefa's nickname], his beloved wife, went insane when she found out his sentence. Completely beside herself, she wrote a good-bye letter to her noble husband and managed to send it to him; several family members had to carry her to the countryside with her children, and there, on the day of the execution, she escaped and started to run through the plains toward Puerto Príncipe, wanting to be reunited with her husband. It took a great effort for her relatives to catch her and carry her back to the estate."[20] When she regained her sanity, Josefa had turned into an old woman, so white was her hair, so wrinkled her face. Her property was confiscated, and she moved with her two children to New York, where she died in December, 1868, at age forty-eight.[21]

After the execution of Joaquín de Agüero, entire clans left Puerto Príncipe and went into voluntary exile. The men of Camagüey planted four palm trees in the town's main square to honor the fallen rebels. The women showed their grief and solidarity with the rebels' widows by collectively dressing in black and cutting their hair short. A popular hymn in the eastern provinces put it this way:

The Camagüeyan woman
who did not cut her hair
does not deserve in this land
to be called a sister.[22]

In 1851, cutting one's hair short had become such a powerful emblem of rebellion that its impact could be felt on the far-western end of the island.

Magdalena Peñarredonda was only a girl when the news of the Camagüeyan women's cutting their hair reached her parents' coffee plantation in Pinar del Río. As soon as Magdalena and her sisters heard the news, they emulated the women of Camagüey and cut off their braids. Their father, a Spaniard, was so furious that he locked them up at home, even refusing to allow them to attend church, until their hair grew back.[23]

These were signs of things to come. The Agüero rebellion had shown that Cubans were not ready for a revolutionary war, but seeds of discontent had been planted on fertile ground. As Cubans' cultural and political identity took shape, hostility toward the colonial power deepened. The signs of resistance the female population displayed in the first half of the nineteenth century, mostly symbolic in nature, revealed women's growing political consciousness. The women's actions, their efforts to highlight the differences between themselves as Cubans and the Spaniards, both reflected and widened the gap between the two societies. In the following decade, women's involvement would move beyond symbolic gestures and enter the realm of politics.

4

▲▼▲▼▲

The Ten Years War
(1868–1878)

The Ten Years War began in Oriente in October, 1868, and gradually spread to the other eastern provinces without ever reaching the western, and richest, part of Cuba. That the rebellion succeeded mainly in this part of the island should come as no surprise.

After the fall of Spain's Bourbon monarchy, the fiscal policies of a new liberal government in Madrid hurt the cattle and agricultural interests of areas such as Camagüey, but left unscathed the owners of the large western and central sugar plantations. The eastern elites who, as previously noted, owned only small numbers of slaves, and often only domestic ones, had little to gain by maintaining the colonial system. Unlike their western counterparts, they could do without the help of the Spanish army, the instrument slaveholders counted on to prevent slave revolts. The eastern region was also home to the island's largest population of free blacks, who naturally had no loyalty to Spain.

By the late 1860s, the antigovernment sentiment that the eastern provinces had displayed erratically in earlier decades reached new heights. In *sociedades*, Masonic lodges, *tertulias* (conversation groups), and family gatherings, Creole society articulated its vision of a new Cuba.

Carlos Manuel de Céspedes, who led the revolt that set off the Ten Years

War, embodied the liberal values of the eastern elite in all its passion and am-biguity. Céspedes, a well-educated liberal and a Mason, and a small group of collaborators declared themselves at war with Spain in October, 1868, at Yara, Oriente. The rebellion was supported by would-be capitalists who felt crippled by the limitations of a rigid colonial system. The rebels' demands included free trade and the right to elect their own representatives to a national assembly. They also asked to be admitted to the United States, a request the American government considered but rejected on the basis that the Cuban population was racially mixed and overwhelmingly Catholic. Given that the rebel leaders made this petition three years after the end of the American Civil War, annex-ation would have meant the abolition of slavery in Cuba. Céspedes freed his own slaves on the day of his pronouncement, yet his movement's official plat-form, issued at Yara, called for gradual abolition—after compensating the slave owners, a gesture meant to attract needed support from property owners.

A few months later, in April, 1869, when forces from all the insurgent ar-eas—Oriente, Camagüey, and Las Villas—gathered at the Constitutional As-sembly of Guáimaro, the new Cuban republic approved a constitution that included the abolition of slavery.

As citizens of the new insurgent society, the former slaves were entitled to their freedom, but only to a point. They were also obligated to work and fight for the rebel cause. The Mambí government, as Rebecca Scott has shown, ex-pected the emancipated women to work as unpaid domestics for wealthy rebel families or to work as agricultural laborers. The women, however, had differ-ent plans and, to the authorities' dismay, often chose to follow the soldiers.[1]

Despite its limitations, the Guáimaro Constitution set free thousands of men and women and forced the Spanish government, in July, 1870, to pass the Moret law. This law emancipated slaves under eleven and over sixty, as well as those who fought with the Spanish army.[2]

Evidence showing that one could favor the rebellion and still cling to one's slaves is to be found in the letters of complaint many wealthy women filed with colonial authorities who had confiscated their property as punishment for their political involvement. A common request was to ask the government to at least return their slaves. Women complained of the hardship of life without the service of their loyal slave Agustina, Francisco, or Leoncio.[3] Government offi-cials were often sympathetic to pleas that they considered reasonable, unless the woman asked for the return of an excessive number of servants. Teresa de Céspedes from Puerto Príncipe was allowed to recover four slaves, rather than the six she had requested.[4]

Despite the inconsistency that plagued the rebels' views of slavery, their official declaration against bondage encouraged black Cubans to side with them and make the insurgency their own cause. The ranks of the Mambí army were soon filled with soldiers of African descent.

When the war broke out, thousands of women were thrown into the conflict. Whether or not they supported the insurgency, once their male relatives joined the rebel forces it became imperative for the women, who, as the wives, daughters, and sisters of the men fighting Spain, were guilty by association, to leave their homes and go along. As Mirta Aguirre puts it, these were "family wars."[5] But it would be inaccurate to define women's relation to the insurgency as their merely being caught in the conflict by domestic circumstances. Women's active participation in the rebellion often grew out of their involvement in their communities. As members of an intricate network of neighbors, friends, and relatives, they developed a collective political identity that informed their ideas and actions.

When the Ten Years War began, towns and rural communities received with excitement the news of the imminent uprising and set to work. Rebel leader Gonzalo de Quesada, referring to Bayamo, wrote: "Young people were enthusiastic about going to war. At night, the agitators met quietly in friendly houses; the women took their best silks, embroidered rosettes for their fiancées, and, combining the three colors of Agüero and López, made blue, white, and red banners."[6]

Adriana del Castillo, a teenager at the time, was among the women who helped her town prepare for the war. During the day, she was active in the Sociedad Filarmónica, a social center where Cubans celebrated Creole traditions and customs. At night, Adriana led a group of young women who, moving from one home to another as a safety precaution, produced bandages and other war equipment.[7]

Ten days after Céspedes rose up in arms against the Spanish Crown, the rebel army took the city of Bayamo and founded *el gobierno en armas* (republic in arms). At first, it all seemed like a game, a patriotic and inspirational play put on by a familiar cast that included friends and relatives. Candelaria Figueredo, a friend of Adriana del Castillo, was sixteen at the time. She was born in 1852 and was the daughter of "Perucho" Figueredo, a rebel hero. She grew up in an antigovernment environment, her home often serving as a center for the insurgent conspirators. In her autobiography, she recounts her excitement at being named standard-bearer for the rebel forces in Bayamo. Her father enlisted her participation by announcing: "My daughter Candelaria will dare."[8]

Her friends and sisters immediately set to work making Candelaria attire fit for the occasion—a white Amazonian dress, a Phrygian liberty cap, and a tri-color flag, an interesting symbiosis of French and Cuban revolutionary sym-bols. Dressed in this outfit, and proudly carrying the flag, she led the insurgent soldiers through the streets of Bayamo as the population cheered.[9]

Bayamo remained in rebel hands for three months, and during this time the local press reflected the insurgents' aspirations. On January 1, 1869, the insur-gent paper *Cubano Libre* published an appeal to the town's youth to arm them-selves, fight for their country, and defend the "sacred codes of freedom and independence." The call ended with a revolutionary "Allons enfants de la patrie/le jour de gloire est arrivé" (Arise, children of the fatherland/the day of glory has arrived) and was signed by "Varias Bayamesas" [Several women from Bayamo], probably the group led by Adriana del Castillo.[10] As Benedict Ander-son has pointed out, newspapers were one of the crucial tools nineteenth-century nationalist movements could use to promote their agenda.[11] With their appeal, these young women were connecting their fight to the Enlighten-ment and the French Revolution and encouraging their compatriots to join in the birth of a new society.

Soon, however, it became impossible to keep the Spanish army at bay, and the early enthusiasm gave way to realization of the rebels' tenuous position. Determined not to allow government forces to benefit from their impending victory, the people of Bayamo abandoned their town after setting it on fire. Men and women, young and old, left to hide in the thick forests of the region. Their life on the run had begun. With it came a new awareness that this was no game. Candelaria recounts the increasing difficulties they met: "We began to suffer a thousand vicissitudes, but the first year it was all right because there were country estates, with good houses and plenty of food; but in early 1870, the situation became more difficult for the families, especially because the en-emy burned and destroyed everything in its path."[12]

Burning fields would become a constant feature of this war, with tragic consequences. As the war escalated and more rebels hid in the countryside, the Spanish government, to prevent support for the insurgency, ordered the torch-ing of fields belonging to peasants who were suspected of sympathizing with the opposition. The rebels retaliated by burning the land of property owners who were loyal to the authorities. As a result, it was increasingly difficult for rebel families to find food or even to hide. When Candelaria's father became ill with typhoid fever, their situation grew desperate. In August, 1871, govern-ment soldiers found the family and took them prisoner, but Candelaria man-aged to escape. Lost in the mountains she tried to find traces of her family without success:

I returned to the forest and, in a torrential rain, I sat underneath a tree. There I spent the cruelest night of my life. Morning had hardly broken when I left the woods again, always watchful for footprints left after the rain of the enemies who had taken my family prisoner; I wandered all day; at sunset I heard someone calling me from the forest; I stopped walking and saw a black woman I knew. Knowing that I wanted to re-unite with my family by any possible means, she advised me not to do so, since the Spanish would kill me, and that would be another blow to my parents. Partly because I feared that she was right, or perhaps because of my sadness at the painful events that had happened, and for lack of food, I fell to the ground and spent the night crying bitterly.[13]

After a few days wandering in the woods, Candelaria found her younger brother and sister, who had also managed to escape, and heard the news of her father's execution. For months Candelaria and her siblings lived a life of hard-ship, barely surviving on raw fruit. They finally joined a rebel brigadier's family that was also in hiding, but not for long. Having women with them who were not used to the physical challenges imposed by an outdoor life put the men in a difficult position. The brigadier "argued, quite rightly, that being with us, with his wife, his sister, and a few other women whom we had encountered in the forest, would cost him his life, because he couldn't bring himself to join his comrades and leave us to starve, since there were days we went without food and we were already extremely weak."[14] The easiest solution was to encourage the women to go back to the towns. As females, they were viewed as innocent and harmless by both the rebels and the colonial power.

This cultural tenet, however, like many others, was shaken by the war. With growing numbers of women taking an active role in defying the gov-ernment, more women became victims of its repression. Having played a visible role as flag carrier, Candelaria felt vulnerable and refused to turn her-self in. Only through trickery and deception were the men in her party able to convince her to leave the mountains, and she soon fell into the hands of Spanish soldiers. She and Borjita Céspedes, sister of Carlos Manuel Céspe-des, president of the rebel Cuban republic, were taken prisoner and jailed in the town of Manzanillo:

The following day, I was led into [Spanish officer] Rodríguez's presence and he asked me if I knew someone who could send us food; I told him that I did not know anyone in Manzanillo.

"How can this be?" he asked me.

"It is easy to understand: I am not from Manzanillo; I am a Bayamesa!"

"With such pride you say this."

"I speak the truth, all the town knows that Pedro Figueredo is from Bayamo."

"All right then," he said to me, "but your father has many friends here."

"That is true, but all those friends went with him to fight in the Revolution."

"Then you will not eat."

"Fine," I said to him with indifference, "but it was my understanding that a government that took a prisoner had to sustain her."

Another official at his side looked at him, and they both smiled; they asked me various questions to which I answered calmly that I did not know. They then took me to prison, and we spent the day without eating and not even having any water to drink, although we tried to take some from a carafe that was there, but that was impossible. It had a nauseating flavor, and poor Borjita, who could not endure the thirst, drank a little. It made her sick and she vomited.[15]

Candelaria's physical conditions improved a few days later when a friend of her father sent food. Finally, in October, 1871, she was freed and forced into exile in Florida, where surviving family members had settled. She was luckier than many other Bayamo refugees. Adriana del Castillo, among many others, died of typhoid fever while hiding in the mountains.

Candelaria Figueredo's participation in the revolutionary struggle was intimately linked to her position as the daughter of a rebel leader, as seen in the way she signed her autobiography: "Candelaria Figueredo (Perucho's daughter.)" But her role as flag carrier and the defiance she exhibited in prison suggest that she strongly identified, at least at an emotional level, with the anticolonial struggle. This combination of a political position, defined through ties to a male relative, and a steely personal determination to be part of the rebellion characterizes Cuban women's participation in the Ten Years War.

The same duality can be found in Manuela Cancino's wartime ordeal. Like Candelaria Figueredo, Manuela Cancino experienced the Ten Years War, with her sisters Micaela and Mercedes, as a daughter of a revolutionary Cuban leader. Manuela was born in 1848, and her merchant family left Florida after

England acquired it in 1763 and settled in Bayamo. When the war broke out, Manuela's father, a colonel in the rebel army, took his family to the Sierra Maestra, which was controlled by revolutionary forces. They remained there throughout the conflict. Manuela and her family lived in several of those "little nameless hamlets," described by James O'Kelly, the reporter for the New York *Herald*, as "a numerous class of settlements scattered over Cuba Libre."[16]

A crucial element for the survival of the rebellion in the 1870s was the establishment of *talleres*, or workshops, throughout the rebel territory, most of which were run by women. In addition to shouldering the responsibility of cultivating the fields and taking care of the cattle, women, with the help of injured men, organized these small communities, hidden deep in the mountains, that produced weapons, horseshoes, saddles, and other war supplies needed by the rebels. O'Kelly described these settlements for his American readers: "It was to me extremely interesting to watch this germ of a new society. Their manufactures are confined to the chief necessities of life. The cotton-tree gives pods that are skillfully spun into threads; the majajua, twine, from which hammocks, sandals, shoes even, are made, as well as those most useful sacks in which the patriot often carries a crop he has reaped, though he has not sown it; and many kinds of grasses are woven into sombreros to shelter patriot heads from the fierce ardor of the sun. These manufactures are carried on by women."[17]

Manuela Cancino and her sisters grew up breathing the ideal of independence and sharing with soldiers the trials and tribulations of a life on the move. In 1872, they found themselves encamped in El Ranchito, a small rebel enclave in a remote part of the mountains, where they lived undisturbed by the enemy. There they grew vegetables, staffed a hospital for sick and wounded Mambí soldiers, and built a school.[18] Three other young women, also daughters of rebel officers, had taken refuge at the same camp, making the Cancino sisters' daily life more bearable. When the Mambí government set up camp nearby, a group of young officers found their way to visit them. These young people were not strangers to each other: they belonged to the same social set, and their ties were made stronger by the revolutionary struggle. They spoke to each other informally, as old friends and comrades, yet maintained the boundaries of propriety that nineteenth-century society, revolutionary or not, deemed necessary.

Among the visiting soldiers was the poet Fernando Fornaris. As was often done, he was asked to improvise a poem. So with a candle in his hand, Fornaris, stanza by stanza, sang the virtues of the six girls, their celestial beauty, their sweet timidity, their pure innocence. He later copied the verses in Micaela Cancino's album, which she had kept from childhood and throughout the Ten Years War:

In this elevated land
refuge of the Cuban people
where the Spanish never
have set down their bold soles,
there is a hill buried deep between the highest
mountains, where among flowers and canes
without fears or care,
lives an honest family
beneath rustic shacks.
There the revolution's impetus sent this family
and since then it felt its situation improve.
Model of abnegation
and of sainted Christian faith,
in this inhumane war
that despotism sustains
with valiant patriotism
it serves the Cuban cause.
Tied to this family
there are six virtuous
pure, cheerful, beautiful girls
whom the world has forgotten.
Even the fairies are jealous
of their grace and delicacy;
so much splendor pours forth,
their beauty is so unequalled
that in my tropical land
they are the queens of love.[19]

Most of the officers who visited the girls in El Ranchito, including the poet, died in the war. All the girls, not surprisingly, married army officers. Manuela, the most committed to the revolutionary cause, became a poet and a teacher. We shall find her fighting the colonial power again in the 1890s.

Concha Agramonte's experience illustrates how abruptly the war could change women's lives, particularly if they were wealthy. When the rebellion began, the sheltered and, in some cases, opulent lifestyle of some women of the eastern provinces came to an end. Within months, or even days, they moved from the comfort of their mansions to a precarious life on the run.

Concha Agramonte was born in 1834 in Puerto Príncipe to one of the wealthiest families in the eastern provinces. Antique furniture, chandeliers, marble, mirrors, china, and silver decorated her parents' palatial home. She grew up wearing delicate silk and lace and being waited on by slaves. As a young woman, Concha and her sisters wore jewels so valuable that they were escorted to dances and concerts by armed and mounted guards. Bored and locked up at home with nothing much to do—particularly during the rainy season—Concha spent innumerable hours in her father's library reading nationalist literature.

The Agramontes responded to the Agüero uprising and the resulting executions in the same manner as Camagüey's other leading families: in protest, they closed the doors to their house in town and moved to their country estate to spend several months in mourning. And like other Camagüeyan women, Concha, her mother, and her sisters cut their hair. A year later, in 1852, Concha Agramonte married Francisco Sánchez Betancourt, another member of the island's eastern elite. For her wedding, a rug covered the road from her home through the town's square and to the church door; thousands of candles lighted the way. Francisco's wealth allowed her to continue living in opulence. Concha reportedly followed the fashion dictated by the French empress, Eugénie; her skirts used more than thirty meters of cloth, and she possessed the most valuable emeralds and other jewelry.[20]

In 1868, the Ten Years War began, and the Sánchez Agramontes sided with the rebel forces. In fact, Concha's husband was a member of the Camagüey Revolutionary Committee and actively participated in the Camagüey Assembly of 1869. Leaving their town residence, the family took refuge at Juan Gómez, their country estate, which became a well-known rebel meeting place. "With their arrival in the countryside, the face of the revolution changed in Camagüey," explained rebel writer Luis Lagomasinos. "They gave shelter daily to more than one hundred people."[21]

In the early months of the rebellion, the Cuban forces, still strong and filled with optimism, incongruously, kept up the social practices to which they were accustomed. Concha presided over lavish parties and banquets, as she had done in peacetime. In November, 1869, after a dinner attended by the top representatives of the rebel government, one of the guests improvised a poem in honor of the hostess and "queen of the party." Birds lost their bright plumage in winter, he said, trees, their leaves, the sun's rays, their warmth; everything changed except "Conchita," who was always flowery spring.[22]

Not all rebels experienced such a glamorous existence. Insurgent society was still divided by class and race. White upper-class women whose relatives joined the rebellion were likely to take shelter in comfortable country homes owned by their families or friends. Ana Betancourt, for example, spent time hiding in Amalia Simoní's family's country state, La Matilde, as well as taking refuge at her friend Concha Agramonte's estate, Juan Gómez. The three women came from well-connected, affluent Camagüeyan families. By contrast, former slaves and poor peasants, unable to rely on such networks, had to settle more often than not for precarious living arrangements in caves and primitive *bohíos*, or huts.

Yet the war swept away some of those social differences and acted as a unifying force. For one thing, the rebel army soon became the most integrated structure on the island. When black and white soldiers and officers mingled and interacted in the *manigua*, so did their female relatives. A soldier, Ramón Roa, mentions in his war memoir how he was once sent to a country house in Camagüey to recover from an illness. There he found Bernarda Toro, Máximo Gómez's wife, who was white, and María Cabrales, Antonio Maceo's wife, who was black, running a makeshift hospital, with no doctors, no medicine, and little food. Both women, working hand-in-hand, helped Roa recover quickly.[23]

As the insurgents increasingly were hunted by the colonial army, the white elite lost the privileges it was accustomed to enjoying. Such was the case of Concha Agramonte. Late in 1869, their safety threatened, she and her family had to flee their home, when the oldest of Concha's eleven children was not yet fifteen years old. For a while they settled in the village of Guáimaro, the capital of the revolutionary government. When the Spanish army laid siege to Guáimaro, the rebels decided to burn it down, as they had done with Bayamo.

Moving from one place in the *manigua* to another, Concha and her family were tracked by the Spanish army. From village to village they went, often sleeping outside, an ordeal made more difficult by Concha's pregnancy. She gave birth to her daughter Sara in the woods, not far from where her husband and older sons were fighting (and where one of them died in combat).

Finally, they were caught by a Spanish patrol in 1871. The Spanish officer in charge, who knew her family, agreed to give her an eight-day safe pass to leave Cuba. Accompanied by most of her children and a few servants, she traveled through the mountains in the midst of torrential rains, first to Puerto Príncipe and then Havana. Concha hid some of her jewelry in her children's belts during their long journey across Cuba and was able to outwit the Spanish soldiers who subjected the family to ferocious searches. They were allowed to depart for New York, but only after she suffered a severe nervous breakdown. Once in the United States, where she was later joined by her husband, she sold the jewelry to Tiffany's and took a job as a seamstress. Eventually, she established her own small dressmaking shop and hired other Cuban women who were in a similarly difficult situation.[24]

Concha Agramonte's political involvement had a variety of roots. Many members of her Puerto Príncipe milieu, her friends and relatives, opposed Spanish rule, which they considered unjust and confining both politically and financially. After her husband joined the rebellion, she could hardly have avoided being targeted by the government. Yet Concha Agramonte was not simply caught up in the war by social circumstances. She strongly identified with the anticolonial movement and continued to be politically active after her husband's death and well into her sixties.

When trying to understand the rebel women's participation in the anticolonial war, it is useful to think of nationalism in the broad sense, as defined by Benedict Anderson. Nationalism is not, he argues, a specific political agenda one can put in writing and discuss, but, rather, a cultural artifact, part of a large cultural system that includes points of view, longings, and half-consciously held beliefs.[25] The roots of Concha Agramonte's support for the rebellion lay in something as concrete as the love of her family and as intangible as her vision of a free Cuba. The ideological and cultural values associated with the rebellion became instrumental in defining who she was. From a contemporary perspective, the ideals the insurgency embodied seem ambiguous and unfocused, but to the men and women fighting for them, they were meaningful enough to be worth great sacrifice. This was also the case with Concha Agramonte's friend Amalia Simoní.

Amalia Simoní, the wife of Ignacio Agramonte, one of the top military leaders of the Ten Years War, spent her honeymoon on the battlefield. Amalia and Ignacio were married on August 2, 1868, and he joined the rebels the following November. An avid fan of Victor Hugo and Lamartine, authors he read despite their being censored, Ignacio was the epitome of the romantic hero—young, handsome, and brave. Amalia, too, was full of nineteenth-century virtues. She was plump, beautiful, a talented singer, and better educated and more cosmopolitan than most women of her generation.

When Ignacio joined the rebels, Amalia went into hiding at La Matilde, her parents' country house. Once her safety was threatened, she and her relatives abandoned this refuge and fled into the woods. Ignacio found a clearing in a thick forest and there, with palm trees, they built a little ranch they called El

Idilio (The Romance), where their first child was born. As was the case for Candelaria Figueredo and Concha Agramonte, the early years of the rebellion, though not easy, were bearable for Amalia. Despite her comfortable background, she seemed able to adjust to her new circumstances. Ignacio, writing to his mother, already in exile, indicated that his wife accepted the new and nomadic living conditions as a worthy sacrifice:

> Amalia enjoys good health. She's had a few scares, at times some discomfort and privation, but she is happy. Most of the time she lives on some ranch in the forest with [her father] Simoní and with [her sister] Manuela, while I am fighting the campaign. There they lack countless of those small things that we don't appreciate in the towns because they are so common. They patch their dresses because there is no way to repair them. However, [Amalia] thinks that none of this is as important as freeing Cuba. She carries on with pleasure, dreaming of our triumphs and trying to get news from the war. Our [son] Ernesto occupies all of her time. She rears him herself, carries him, and attends to him. She is crazy about him.[26]

By 1870, support for the revolution had declined and the presence of Spanish soldiers had increased. Despite Ignacio's military prominence, the Agramontes became vulnerable when the Cuban army's positions deteriorated. Agramonte visited his wife as often as his war responsibilities allowed, and on one of those occasions, the family was surprised by the enemy. Amalia described the incident:

> May 26, 1870, my son's birthday, we woke up happy, preparing to celebrate the first birthday of our firstborn son. We were at El Idilio, my parents, my sister, and her children, and my Ignacio, who was not in very good health and had been with us for five days. That same day, and when we were most happy, a boy arrived at eight in the morning, saying that the Spanish forces were coming toward El Idilio, a warning we never knew who sent. Ignacio did not believe him and, trying to soothe me, told me that it could not be true, because he had no warning from his assistants and the Estado Mayor [central command], which, whenever they came to visit us, stayed less than a mile from us. But a little while later, the same boy returned saying, "The Spanish troops are already near El Idilio." Ignacio, who had the baby in his arms and was laughing when he heard him pronounce so poorly the few words that he knew, became

serious and, embracing his son and me, said with a grave voice, "This seems like treason. Do not upset yourself; the wife of a soldier must be brave." He called to Father and said to him, "Go deep into the mountains with the family; prepare yourselves quickly with only the clothing absolutely necessary and leave here immediately . . . I am going to see what is happening; in any case, I will return within two or three hours.[27]

That was the last time they saw each other. Amalia's family was discovered and taken to Camagüey, where a group of government volunteers wanted to kill the baby because he was Ignacio Agramonte's son. With the help of friends, however, the family was able to leave the island. And so began Amalia Simoní's life in exile, first in New York, where she gave birth to a daughter, and later in Mexico.

In exile, Amalia, who had never worked, supported her family by giving music lessons and concerts. She also received occasional letters from her husband, letters full of revolutionary spirit, hope, love, and anguish. In the final letter Amalia received, Ignacio wrote: "And you, my love, never doubt that I live thinking of you, that my most fervent desire is that we meet never to be parted again, that I do not know any happiness or anything better than your love; that only through your love is life pleasant for me and that the passion, the delirium with which your Ignacio worships you will never change."[28] Less than a year later, Ignacio was killed in battle.

Like Amalia Simoní, Concha Agramonte, Manuela Cancino, and Candelaria Figueredo, thousands of women throughout the Mambí land lived close to the battlefield. Whenever possible, however, men tried to keep their wives and children away from the most vulnerable areas. Families were packed off and sent to safer areas or into exile. Inevitably, lovers took the wives' place. Despite the natural disruption of the war, the revolutionary government attempted from the start to address moral standards. The Guáimaro Chamber, in an affirmation of its liberal inclinations, introduced a civil marriage law as well as legal divorce based on mutual consent. Civil marriages were considered legitimate marriages among the rebel population. These unions took place in front of municipal judges, *prefectos*, who acted as civil servants, and with two witnesses for each participant.[29]

Ignacio Agramonte was the leader perhaps most concerned with maintaining moral standards in the rebel army. Ramón Roa recalled how upset Agramonte became to see one of his officers living with a young woman, despite their not being married: "The major [Ignacio Agramonte] criticized harshly, and in writing, a cavalry commander, a handsome and brave lad, who was well respected by him, as well as by all his fellow soldiers, for inducing a comely girl with whom he had relations, to abandon her maternal house and plan her escape without mediating the celebration of legal marriage as was in use; he argued that the fact that he was the leader of the area where this transgression took place only made his behavior more condemnable."[30]

Ignacio Agramonte's moral preoccupation was genuine and not politically motivated, but upholding high moral standards did indeed grant political benefits. Projecting an aura of respectability was important to an army with an image problem. The rebel army lacked the recognition that starched uniforms, shiny decorations, and elaborate ceremonies normally give the military. The insurgents were poor, and it showed. This made some Cubans, as well as foreign powers and observers, reluctant to take the rebels seriously and offer their support.

But the rebellion's problem was not simply a matter of financial resources. Race was also an issue. While the Ten Years War had begun as a white man's conflict, within a few years thousands of black Cubans had joined the rebellion and risen in the military ranks. Their presence was used by the enemy to challenge the credibility of the Mambí army. Arguing that this was a war of impoverished, half-naked Africans who shared no moral tenets with white Cubans, the Spanish government and Cuban plantation owners attempted, often successfully, to dissuade the Creole population from backing the insurgency.[31] Consequently, to assuage those fears, the rebels accentuated Mambí moral caliber. Presenting themselves as respectable nineteenth-century gentlemen who had the support of their pious mothers, wives, and daughters helped appease the anxiety aroused by a racially and socially mixed army.

Nineteenth-century society excluded women from public life, barring them from the political realm and the workplace. But it also placed them on a higher moral ground than their male counterparts. In Europe and the United States, the ideal of the angelic female was an important cultural tenet. Cuban society, too, celebrated women's moral superiority. The virtuous, pure Cuban woman was an ally that the Mambí cause wanted on its side. Her commitment to rebel ideals demonstrated the holiness of the insurgents' struggle. For was she not, as a woman, a nonpartisan supporter, an apolitical player who merely wanted what was best for her children?

The rebel rhetoric constructed the symbol of the ideal Mambisa and turned this symbol into a useful political instrument. According to the revolutionary rhetoric, the Mambisas' virtues included abnegation, self-sacrifice, and strength in the face of martyrdom. Their role was to remind their male relatives of their military obligations.

Bernarda Toro, the wife of Máximo Gómez, who in the 1890s would become the top military leader of the rebel forces, embodied the true Mambisa's virtues. She was born in Oriente in 1852, and married, at the beginning of the Ten Years War, in the *manigua*. She gave birth in a rebel camp and, as José Martí poetically observed, carried her many children "marching through combats in the cradle of her arms."[32] Like many other rebel women, Bernarda lost babies to the harsh living conditions of the battle camps. When Clemencia, her oldest daughter, was barely a month old, mother and child were left hidden in the mountains with a couple of men to protect them. Surprised by the enemy, Bernarda, barefoot and with the baby in her arms, fled the enemy as the officer and the soldier fought to their deaths. Mother and child were lost in the mountains for two days, without food or water until a rebel party found them.[33]

Bernarda experienced all the negative consequences of her husband's political involvement: life in the woods, prison, exile, poverty, and the death of her oldest son in battle in 1896. But through it all, she maintained a Spartan selflessness that rebel rhetoric held up as a model for other women. Once in exile, Bernarda refused offers of aid from the president of the revolutionary junta in New York, who had heard of the difficult time she was having feeding her children. She proclaimed in response: "Those of us ladies who have given everything to the fatherland do not have time to occupy ourselves with the material needs of existence, it should not be spent on us what should go to pay for gunpowder."[34]

She was also praised for not having burdened her famous husband with petty jealousy, having recognized that, deep in his heart, he loved her, despite appearances to the contrary. (Gómez was famous for his extramarital affairs.) Bernarda Toro, or at least the public persona that the rebels created, became the ideal Mambisa: a woman who never burdened her husband; a woman devoted to her family; and a woman who ultimately would be willing to sacrifice all for a greater cause, *la patria*. Under the adverse conditions the war created, the most valuable woman a man could have was one who adapted to the new circumstances without complaining and who encouraged her children to fight for the cause.

Mambisas were obedient daughters, devoted wives, admiring girlfriends, but, above all, they were mothers. And as mothers, the Mambisas' political potential was fully realized. Symbolizing pure, unselfish love, a mother's role as bearer of soldiers and her willingness to give up her children for *la patria* represented the ultimate testament to the worthiness of the rebel cause.

Luz Vázquez fit this definition of the heroic rebel mother. Luz was born in 1831 in Bayamo to an elite Creole family. A renowned beauty, before the war she lived an opulent existence, filled with dances and gatherings at the town's social center, La Filarmónica, where it is likely that she sharpened her political views and joined in the passionate discussions about Cuba's future. She opened her mansion to celebrate the Cuban victory only a few hours after her oldest son died in the rebel siege of Bayamo.[35] A true Mambisa, she put *la patria* ahead of even her children.

So did the mother of Comm. José Vargas. When her son was condemned by the rebels for treason, she stood in front of those who had tried him. Assuming she wanted to question the decision, members of the jury began to explain the need to abide by the law. "I did not come here to ask for clemency for my son," she interrupted. "If he was a traitor, he is well dead, and may God forgive him. I have two children left: They are serving their country, they are my pride, but if they betray Cuba, I will not cry for their deaths."[36]

Yet in the role of revolutionary mother, no one surpassed Mariana Grajales. Born in 1808, she was a member of the large class of free mulattoes who worked as craftspeople or, as in the case of her family, small landowners in Santiago and vicinity. She likely received no education and probably could neither read nor write. Married twice, she produced two daughters and, more famously, eleven brave sons who fought and, almost all, died in the war. She is best known as the mother of Antonio Maceo. A brilliant soldier and strategist, Maceo was one of the top military leaders of the Ten Years War and, to this day, is worshiped in Cuba. Maceo used to recall how his mother sang her children antislavery lullabies such as this one:

The ant is born free,
The *bibijagua* (leaf-cutter ant) and the cricket,
Without concerns regarding money,
No Spaniard to pursue them,
Or law obligating them
To go to the notary's office
To buy their freedom,
And I, with my dignity,
Will I not be free someday?[37]

Mariana Grajales. Fondo Cubano, Grajales. Sobre 1, BNJM

As small property owners and free blacks, Mariana and her husband had no reason to support the colonial government. But it was Mariana's passion that brought her family's commitment to the insurgency to an extraordinary level. Jean Stubbs has pointed out how the Escalera conspiracy of 1844 and subsequent repression of people of African descent shaped Grajales's political views. Keeping alive the memories of those events, she made sure her children were aware of the injustice the colonial government had perpetrated.[38] When the Ten Years War broke out, Mariana Grajales was ready. María Cabrales, Antonio's wife, wrote that as soon as the news of the 1868 uprising reached the Maceo family, her mother-in-law, Mariana, fetched a crucifix and, gathering her husband and children around her, asked each to swear they would give their lives for their country.[39] When the Maceo men joined the rebel army, Mariana and her daughters accompanied them. Other women were there as well, mostly the wives and relatives of free blacks and former slaves, who had either run away or been freed by their owners so that they would support the rebellion.

Mariana, then sixty, must have found life on the run strenuous. The key to the safety of the rebel bases was their inaccessibility. Protected by flowing rivers and impenetrable woods, on high mountains or steep cliffs, the insurgents made their homes in some of the most impassable regions of Oriente. They changed camp as often as military needs demanded, and the women followed, living on ranches, in huts or caves. The fighters also reclaimed shelters in the old *palenques*, which were particularly numerous in Oriente. They turned the *palenques* into hospitals, workshops, and refuges.

Mariana's age and charisma, as well as the many sons she had on the front, made her a natural leader. She tended to sick and wounded soldiers, often her own children, cooked for the soldiers, and mended their clothes. She also acted as midwife and nurse. In January, 1869, she assisted her daughter-in-law, María Cabrales, in delivering a son who lived only seven days. A few months later, María's young daughter died, too. This was a life few small children could survive.[40]

Mariana spent ten years in the mountains. During this time she saw her children rise through the ranks of the rebel army and gain the respect of their comrades and enemies alike. Her husband and several of her sons were killed, but Mariana, remarkably, maintained an unflinching commitment to the rebel cause.

José Martí memorialized that dedication twenty years later. Through Martí's writings, Mariana became a symbol of her country's struggle. During his travels to promote the Cuban Revolutionary Party he met her in Jamaica, where she lived in exile after the Ten Years War. He understood that she could stand as a powerful symbol of Cuban nationalism. Strong, brave, and supportive, she was a shining example of heroism that could inspire both men and women. He wrote in *Patria*, the proindependence paper: "It was the day that they brought Antonio Maceo in wounded: he had been shot in the chest. Carried on their shoulders, he was unable to focus, and pale with the color of death. All the women, and there were many, began to cry, some against the wall, others on their knees by the dying man, another in a corner, the broken face in her arms. And his mother, with a scarf on her head, expelled the crying women from the hut, as if scaring away chickens: 'Get out, leave here, skirt-wearers! I will not tolerate any tears.'" Then Martí recounts how Mariana, still mourning the death of one son and with three others wounded, gave her youngest child the command for which she is most famous: "And you, stand tall, it's time for you to go fight for your country."[41]

The nineteenth century had a penchant for grandiose pronouncements that sound contrived to contemporary ears. Did Mariana Grajales really say that? Was Bernarda Toro so undemanding? Luz Vázquez so courageous? Were women so committed to the rebel cause that they would sacrifice their children to this ideal? Have not women throughout history tended to put private concerns—such as the survival of their families—before public ones?

There are several layers to these questions. As the death toll of Cuban patriots rose in the war, the old image of Spain as the homeland faded and was replaced by that of cruel despotism. Aroused by the injustice of the colonial system that denied their communities political representation and freedom, and enraged by the demise of their loved ones, women's antipathy for the colonial authorities led them to act. Believing so strongly in the insurgent cause, but with only limited power to control events, women's display of solidarity with male relatives was a way to affirm their political views and, in the process, vent their anger at the enemy. Their fierce commitment to the revolutionary cause can be viewed as an attempt to fend off the ghost of doubt—to reassure themselves that their losses were not in vain, that their sacrifices were worthwhile.

Mariana Grajales's political determination was, foremost, an expression of her deep commitment to the rebellion, including its rejection of slavery. Her support of the war effort gave her the opportunity to defend the Mambí cause and turned her into a respected public figure. Her bravery might have stemmed also from the need to reassure herself that her children were not dying in vain. Doubts about the wisdom of pursuing a military solution could only lead to fear and self-defeat. Finally, it was only natural for her to hate those responsible for killing her children and to want revenge, no matter the price.

On the other hand, the preternaturally patriotic woman who obsessively encourages her men to fight with little concern for their safety has served as a useful and important resource for military causes throughout history. Take the often told story of the Spartan mother who waited to hear news of the outcome of a battle between Sparta and Athens. When told of the battlefield death of her five sons, she dismissively responded that what she wanted to know was who had won. Hearing that Sparta had prevailed, she rushed to the temple to thank the gods.[42]

Throughout history, as Linda K. Kerber points out in her discussion of women's role in the American Revolution, shaming men has been a standard activity for women in time of war.[43] Carlos Manuel de Céspedes's *Himno Republicano* (*Republican Hymn*) reflects precisely that expectation: "Let the maiden scorn the lover/who does not fly valiantly to fight."[44] Whether or not women displayed such fierce revolutionary determination, believing that they did emboldened the men.

On Mariana Grajales's death in November, 1893, Martí praised her unwavering patriotism and strength. He turned her into a symbol of motherhood for the whole Cuban nation. Grajales, a black woman, was a fitting image to preside over his interracial vision of Cuba Libre. In Martí's imagery, Mariana Grajales, the Cuban family, and *la patria* had become one:

Did she not stand throughout the war, surrounded by her children? Did she not encourage her compatriots to fight, and later heal the wounded Cuban and Spanish soldiers: Did she not, with bleeding feet, follow behind her dying son's stretcher, made from tree branches? And if anyone trembled when coming face to face with his country's enemy, did he not see the mother of Maceo with the scarf on her head, and the tremor stopped! Did she not see her son get up from the stretcher dying of five wounds and with one hand over his mangled entrails and the other hand raised in victory, escape, escorted by agony, down the mountain away from his two hundred pursuers? And she loved, as the best years of her life, the times of hunger and thirst, when every man who arrived at her door made of palms could bring to her news of the death of one of her children. Oh, how she talked, the last time that *la patria* saw her, with shattering words, about the years of the war! . . . In the wreath that *la patria* lays on Mariana Maceo's tomb, one word is written: "Mother!"[45]

Naturally, women did not always behave heroically nor did their presence always help the war effort. If rebel and Spanish sources show evidence of Cuban women's commitment to the insurgency, they also offer proof of their reluctance to support it. On April 28, 1870, a group of Camagüeyan women wrote an open letter calling on their husbands, sons, and brothers to stop fighting. The women argued that war against Spain had brought not the freedom they sought, but devastation for all. Invoking the Spanish heritage that the soldiers on both sides shared, the women's letter encouraged the Cuban rebels to turn themselves in and return to the legality of the Spanish system. It was in the home, with their families, where the ideal of *la patria* could truly be fulfilled: "Do you want liberty? Do you want your country? Then come into our arms and into the peace of the domestic home, and into the love of your children, with whom we will share our last remaining fortune, you will have your country, and you will have liberty. May God once and for all put an end to the fratricidal fight that is devouring us and consuming our country. May there be no winners or losers but, rather, brothers who embrace each other, like children from the same mother."[46]

Other references revealing women's reluctance to sacrifice everything they had for the rebellion come from the mothers who interceded to save their children's lives at any price. When Eduardo Saavedra, a young Cuban rebel who was sick and resting at a *rancho* in Holguín, was taken prisoner and sentenced to die, his mother, devastated, ran to the Spanish authority, the Count of Valmaseda, to ask for clemency for her son. He agreed on the condition that the prisoner perform some services for the government. "The elated mother," recalled a witness, "who at all costs wanted to save her son's life, flew home to her husband, communicating the news and inebriated with happiness. Her husband, a Catalan, an intransigent Spaniard, plain and severe, controlling his emotions, said to her: 'Think of him as already executed, for no son of mine can be a coward or a traitor!' The poor mother, overwrought with pain, saw the solemn prophecy fulfilled."[47]

But even when women supported the rebellion, they could become a hindrance that slowed the soldiers' advance. Women traveled with the army for a number of reasons. Sometimes they were the soldiers' wives or lovers, perhaps pregnant. In other cases, they felt safer with the army than alone in the woods. Or they were members of a soldier's family who had no other place to go. Ramón Roa gives a humorous description of how dangerous it was to cross the *trocha*, the highly fortified zone Spain built to isolate the rebels, when accompanied by the collection of old people and women who had attached themselves to the troops: "Until then we hadn't pondered the number and nature of our nomadic tribe, nor realized that when you added the old people, male and female, the pregnant women, the crippled, the sick, the suckling babies, the women, carrying as they usually do when they can, pots and pans, half-knitted pieces, images of Our Lady of Charity and bottles of honey for 'Cuba Libre,' and the children's food, there were about eighty of us, not counting, of course, a parrot and a famous dog, a hunter of pigs, that also came along."[48]

The key to a successful crossing was absolute silence, as Spanish soldiers made rounds every few miles and watched from towers and forts. Despite the odds against them, this group managed to cross without meeting harm: "We had crossed the *trocha* more successfully than a similar though smaller caravan, which also crossed during the same period, led by Capt. Miguel Rodríguez. When a suckling baby started crying, the leader, nervous about his responsibility or concerned for his safety, shouted, perhaps to give emphasis to his order: 'suffocate that child.' And his mother, a colored woman who as a former slave risked her freedom, or more likely possessed by indescribable terror, pressed the innocent in such a way that he was left dead in her arms!"[49]

In another war classic, *Episodios de la revolución cubana*, Manuel de la Cruz warns that women, with their powers of seduction, can be not merely a burden but also a true threat. In this melodramatic story, Lieutenant Salazar accepts the generous offer of his friend, another rebel officer, to be taken to the man's home so that he can recover from a wound. The friend goes back to fight while Salazar is sweetly nursed by his friend's wife. "It didn't take long for the lieutenant to notice, with growing surprise and deep sorrow, that each day Rosa was being less and less saintly in her pious role as sister of mercy." The officer tries hard to resist the insidious advances of the voluptuous temptress, but "Rosa, with possessed frenzy, determined to have her desires triumph, kept narrowing the invalid's siege, attacking him with refined tenderness." No matter how hard he tried to resist, she would not let him: "Don't leave! I want you to be mine, yes, I want it, I demand it! I'm yours, only yours!" Finally, he gives in, succumbing to her power. After having betrayed his friend, there is only one thing this honorable man can do. He writes in his suicide note: "I have offended you in the most hateful way one can offend a friend, but a remnant of shame compels me to offer you this satisfaction: my cadaver. Salazar."[50]

And yet, despite evidence that the rebel army and women's objectives were not one and the same, the female population's contributions to the colonial cause were clear even to the enemy. Antonio Pirala, a Spanish writer who witnessed the conflict firsthand, wrote in his history of the Ten Years War that women were the most powerful element in favor of the insurrection:

> Cuban women are the ones who have made the insurrection. They were, if not the first ones to feel the affront to their dignity, the first ones to show their indignation. And the opinion the women formed became irresistible to the men. Women spoke without circumspection, plainly and without fear. They spoke to us Spaniards of our excesses, to their people of their unknown rights and their duties. Before the insurrection they got rid of their jewelry to get ammunition; and once the insurrection broke out, just like the matrons of Rome and Sparta, they pointed to it and told relatives "that's where your place is," and they followed them and shared with them the struggle's ups and downs, and all the risks of the outdoors life; or in order to leave the men free and unburdened, they returned to the towns, emaciated, half naked, moribund, some widows, some with orphan babies trying to suck their breast, dry from hunger and sickness.[51]

Cuban women's deep involvement in the rebel cause can be seen in the thousands of documents they, or their relatives on their behalf, filed asking the colonial government to reverse sanctions imposed for participating in illegal activities. Cubans wrote to their local authorities over and over again to have verdicts changed, their protests resulting in voluminous correspondence with the various bureaucratic levels of the colonial government that examined their complaints. The most common request was to ask for a relative's freedom.

Mothers wrote in behalf of their sons and daughters, defending their innocence; children wrote in behalf of their mothers, and so on. In 1870, for example, Gertrudis González de Mendoza, the widow of an infantry commander, explained to authorities that, whereas her dead husband was in favor of the rebellion, their sons, who were in jail, were not politically involved and should be allowed to go.[52] The same year, Francisco Sequeira petitioned to have his mother, Belén Pérez, who had been accused of attacking the government, released from Las Recogidas jail.[53]

One bone of contention was the practice of putting Cubans who were suspected of political involvement under police watch. Once the colonial authorities had identified a person as *infidente,* or disloyal to the Crown, they assigned the suspect the status of *vigilado,* or "under surveillance," and had this title stamped on the person's official papers. This stigma limited the person's ability to travel and made it difficult to find employment, a residence, and so on. Women urged government agents to eliminate this label from their daughters,' their sons,' or their own papers. In some instances, their requests were granted. In the case of María de Jesús Baluja, who came from a rebel family, it was her husband who appealed to have his wife's surveillance lifted, arguing, "Children should not pay for their parents' faults."[54]

A more severe punishment for antigovernment activity was to seize the rebel's property, including the home and land. Confiscation reveals clearly how the war was an intricately woven family affair. When the colonial authorities confiscated a rebel's possessions, it affected not merely the rebel's life but also that of his or her dependents and relatives, who would then try to get the lost property back. In most cases, men were the ones accused of political disloyalty after they joined the rebellion and left their wives, mothers, or daughters with few or no resources. Women filed hundreds of requests to have their property restored. They claimed their menfolk were innocent or, if they had been killed in the war, that death should be punishment enough. One argument often made was that the assets taken from a husband included his wife's dowry, which belonged to her and not to him. Another argument presented was that the property had been sold to a new owner before being confiscated. The relatives of Luisa de Letamendi, a wealthy rebel woman whose seized assets included a plantation and numerous shares in railway companies and banks, claimed that she had recently sold her property to her brothers and that they, and not she, were then the legitimate owners.[55]

Deportation was another penalty the government used against rebel men and women. In 1870, Ana Morales, from San Juan de los Remedos, wrote to the captain general requesting that he lift the banishment of her three daughters to Pinar del Río. The young women were accused of disloyalty, including sending food and letters to their father, who was fighting with the rebels. When the government refused to comply with the mother's request, the eldest daughter, who was twenty-four years old, wrote to petition that they at least be transferred to Havana, where it would be easier to support themselves doing piecework, their only means of survival and a job that was very poorly paid in Pinar del Río.[56]

In another case, the authorities of Sancti Spíritu considered deporting Rosario Castillo, married to a rebel, to serve as a lesson to the whole community. But they abandoned this idea when they realized that she had fourteen children under her charge and practically no resources. Officials allowed her to stay, but under police surveillance.[57]

A common way for women to help the insurgent cause was by working as nurses. During the war, women nursed the sick and wounded under the most inauspicious circumstances and at great risk to themselves. Caridad Bravo, a black woman from Holguín, working as a team with her two daughters in Mayarí, became famous for always knowing when and where the rebels would need her services. Fernando Figueredo, a rebel officer, admiringly described how these women helped Lieutenant Colonel Ríus, who had been wounded in an ambush: "That very night, as Ríus lay suffering from acute pains and the blood had run for many hours from his injury, the mother and her daughters resolved to operate on the wounded man. With the assistance of Lt. Pedro Calas and with a magnificent surgical kit whose instruments consisted merely of a pair of sewing scissors and a bobby pin, they succeeded in extracting the bullet implanted in his hand, sparing the wounded man from incredibly sharp pains, a hemorrhage, and perhaps even death."[58]

Another rebel fighter, Ramón Roa, believed that women's familiarity with the healing properties of plants and herbs was crucial to the recovery of many sick soldiers. Lacking access to quinine and other medication, the insurgent women "concocted creams, salves, and ointments, ingeniously relying on the pharmacopoeia of our varied and inexhaustible flora."[59]

Nurses sometimes shared the fate of their patients, as illustrated by the example of a woman known as Doña Cirila, "indistinctly housekeeper, confidant, and sister of charity to the revolutionaries."[60] Doña Cirila ran a little hospital for Mambí soldiers deep in the mountains. Rebel officer Manuel Sanguily and two other men were brought to her hospital after being wounded. When the Spanish army surprised them, both the men and their nurse were taken prisoner. And when Ignacio Agramonte's rescue operation freed the rebels, Doña Cirila was freed, too.

Dominga Moncada, the mother of the famous Gen. Guillermo Moncada, was another nurse drawn into the conflict. Dominga was born in Santiago to a family of free blacks, whose women were familiar with natural medicine and renowned as midwives. Dominga and her daughter Felipa worked as nurses and emissaries for the rebels in the eastern mountains.[61] Known as the general's mother and a supporter of the rebellion, Dominga Moncada was often harassed by the Spanish authorities and on several occasions jailed in the Castillo del Morro in Santiago.

The most revered nurse of the Ten Years War was Rosario Castellanos, a former slave. Also known as Rosa "la Bayamesa," she included Máximo Gómez, the war's top military leader, among her admirers. Ramón Roa recounts a visit to Rosa's hospital in the company of Gómez. While she prepared her visitors a Cuba Libre—honey she had taken from a beehive mixed with lemon—and a delicious meal of meat, tomatoes, chiles, and sweet potatoes, one of the hospital's patients told them Rosa's story:

> Rosa the Bayamesa was active, nervous, intelligent, and a lover of her Cuban fatherland. When in the year 1871 it seemed that the sky would crumble upon the revolution in Camagüey, she was forced to flee persecution and had to change locations incessantly. Prudence, as well as self-interest, would have recommended that she leave the fight because there was no ammunition, not even machetes. But she never abandoned the wounded and the sick, whom she healed and protected, regardless of their race. Armed with an old carbine and several cartridges she had chanced upon, she watched for the enemy, and when he threatened the vicinity of her charges, she fired into the air; the detonation sounded the alarm and all would take refuge and hide. She climbed trees, opened the beehives, harvested the honey, and saved the wax; because of this she was never short of salves, ointment, and candles for the sick. She shot the cattle, quartered the beef, and her sick ate meat. She concentrated potash from green wood for her rifle, which reddened the ramrod. With the greatest care, she washed wounds and ulcers with vegetable lotions, experimenting at the request of invalids desperate with pain; and she sewed, cooked, mended, and patched the scarce clothing, maintaining everyone's spirits, without ever compromising her vigilance. She was a true sister of charity, with neither prayers nor scapulary.[62]

In addition to women who, like Rosario Castellanos, made it their job to care for the rebel army, the help of the local peasant population was crucial for survival in a war where the environment could be so inhospitable. The soldiers had to deal with all sorts of obstacles nature threw at them—impassable terrain, malaria, torrential rains, heat, and the like. *Guajiros*, as Cuban peasants were known, were mostly of Spanish ancestry. Perfectly attuned to their surroundings, *guajiros* could guide soldiers through the thickest parts of the woods without losing their way and provide the roots, berries, and venison that kept the armies from starving.

Dispersed throughout the island, often in remote, isolated locations, Cuban peasants tended to live a quiet existence. The fertility of the land allowed them to feed their large families adequately without having to resort to others for much help. Eliza McHatton Ripley, the wife of a southern plantation owner who, like many of her class, fled the American South after the Civil War and took refuge in Cuba, commented with Protestant dismay on the *guajiros'* lack of enterprising initiative: "The men were employed in hauling our produce to the depot for shipment from December until May; the remainder of the year they did nothing but attend their own patches, and one man could easily have done all that and had time to spare. During the summer, when pressed for plowmen, we made frequent tempting overtures to them, which they invariably refused. The women raised chickens, but none for sale; fattened hogs, but they were for home consumption; and braided a few Panama hats for their husbands and sons."[63]

By necessity, *guajiros* learned to be self-reliant and to eye officialdom with suspicion. The colonial government heavily taxed them, but did little else. They had to endure poor roads, no access to education, exclusion from administrative positions, and no real opportunities for improving their living conditions. The war forced this generally tranquil population to take sides. But they did not go to join the war; the war came to them. With their land trampled on and burned, Cuban peasants could not remain neutral. Which side they chose to support often depended on where they lived, how long their families had been on the island, and how they had interacted with the colonial government. By and large, however, the rural inhabitants supported the insurrection.

The Spanish had reason to fear that the peasants would support the insurgents in the form of food, weapons, or simply information. In response, the Spanish government issued the following proclamation on April 4, 1869, to the "Habitantes de los Campos" [rural population]: "All men, ages fifteen and up, found beyond a farm shall be shot unless justifiable motives for their violation

are provided. All women not found on their respective farms or in their dwell-
ings or in the houses of their relatives shall be concentrated in the towns of
Jiguaní and Bayamo, where they will be given food and shelter; those who do
not cooperate shall be moved by force."[64]

The penalty for helping the rebels was severe. Ramón Roa recounts an incident in which a Cuban guerrilla working for the Spanish army caught several
peasant families aiding the enemy. The men were taken away and "the women
purposely abandoned naked on the Camino Real; undoubtedly as a warning to
the families living in the woods."[65] But support from the *guajiros* continued.
Roa also describes how, when he found refuge in a peasant family's home, a
young woman came to his rescue at a moment when he was exhausted, sick,
and starving: "A daughter of Lemus who was keeping a chicken, the only fowl
in the house, with extraordinary care until she had her child, since the time
for her lying in was near, without consulting anyone, with generous instinct,
sacrificed the bird in my honor and then served me the broth with salt and
mint."[66] On another occasion, he was thrilled to get some tobacco from a
young *guajira* in exchange for a poem she asked him to compose for her: "Virgin of Charity/Divine Lady/We ask for Cuba's Freedom/Without delay," he
wrote to the young woman's delight.[67]

What exactly Cuba's freedom meant for these young *guajiras* is hard to determine. But it is clear that, in the context of the war, small, individual gestures
such as feeding a hungry soldier or providing him with tobacco were full of
political significance. When possible, both in rural and urban communities,
women took these individual actions to a collective realm by forming clandestine groups to help the insurgency.

Cuban women's most effective vehicle for supporting the war effort was the
club or association. The rebel government recognized their potential early on,
as is seen in proclamations such as one from 1869 calling the women of Las
Villas—addressed as *ciudadanas* (citizens)—to fulfill their sacred duty and
support the insurrection by organizing themselves to take care of the sick, sew
uniforms, and encourage the men to be brave.[68]

During the Ten Years War, women joined revolutionary groups to aid the
rebel cause. Clubs allowed women, who were far from the battlefield, to participate in the war while performing familiar domestic activities, such as sewing and cooking, though infused now with meaning and excitement. The clubs
accommodated different degrees of involvement among the women, a flexible arrangement that suited their various levels of political commitment. All
members, however, were sworn to secrecy and were given a wartime pseud-

onym to be used when involved in revolutionary activity. Joining a club was a risky affair: many women went to jail when their membership was discovered. Some groups had a mixed composition of men and women, but not the majority. Women, for the most part, worked with other females, an arrangement they found more comfortable and proper. As members of these organizations, they occupied positions of responsibility and entered the political arena of their country. Thus women were offered an opportunity to exercise, even though illegally, the rights of citizenship.

During the Ten Years War, Cuban women helped create a new set of values and practices that allowed the rebellion to last as long as it did. Whether they met secretly with other women to assist the war effort, wrote revolutionary appeals in the newspaper, worked in production centers, or nursed wounded soldiers in hidden *palenques*, the Mambisas' political input helped sustain the revolutionary effort. Two figures, Emilia Casanova and Ana Betancourt, deserve special attention for their role in carving a political niche for Cuban women during the war.

5

▲▼▲▼▲

Mambisas as Citizens

Emilia Casanova and Ana Betancourt

Emilia Casanova deserves credit for creating the blueprint of the Cuban woman's club. She was born in Cárdenas in 1832 to a wealthy slaveholding family and, as a young woman, led the privileged life of the Cuban upper classes. She enjoyed reading French novels, dancing, and horseback riding. And as it had on many others of her generation, Narciso López's failed invasion in 1850 and subsequent execution made a deep impression on Emilia: "I was still a child when, on a morning in May, the brave Narciso López planted the flag he had designed to symbolize Cuba's freedom and independence in front of the window of my house in Cárdenas. I thought the flag so beautiful, so great the man who carried it that, from that moment, I swore to myself I would consecrate my life to that sacred and noble goal."[1]

Today, it is hard to understand López's magnetism. His heroic crusade was meant to bring Cuba into the arms of the United States as one more southern slaveholding state. But for Emilia Casanova and her contemporaries, López represented not the American slaveholders who financed his filibustering venture but someone willing to die fighting the Spanish domination.

An oft-repeated anecdote recounts how, at age twenty, Emilia attended a dinner where several Spanish authorities were present. When the time for toasts arrived, raising her glass, she said pleasantly: "I toast the world's happiness. And furthermore, Cuba's independence," thus bringing the occasion to an abrupt end.[2]

She married Cirilo Villaverde, the author of *Cecilia Valdés* and one of the most important nineteenth-century Cuban writers, who lived in exile because of his involvement with the annexationist cause. They spent most of their married life in the United States. In 1868, husband and wife were thrilled to see the Ten Years War break out. "Here's the revolution," announced Emilia when she heard news about Yara. "Welcome. We are now free."[3]

From New York, where they were active members of the émigré community, the couple gave the rebels' cause their full support. Emilia became the editor of *América Latina*, a paper that advocated severing ties with Spain. In January, 1869, in New York, she founded the first political group ever organized by a Cuban woman, the League of Cuba's Daughters (Liga de las Hijas de Cuba), which was highly successful at raising funds to buy gunpowder, weapons, and medicine for the rebel army. In March of that year, for instance, the group sold tickets to a play and brought in more than $4,000 for the insurgency. All the while, she was rearing a family. Her husband wrote: "The fact of enjoying a comfortable position and of belonging to a social class which, as a general rule, is not known for its maternal tenderness, has not prevented her from breast feeding her three children."[4]

Emilia's self-confidence was extraordinary for a nineteenth-century woman —Cuban or not. She never hesitated to ask high-ranking U.S. government officials to aid the Cuban cause. When her father was taken prisoner by the Spanish authorities, Emilia telegraphed Secretary of State Hamilton Fish asking for help. She then wrote to Domingo Dulce, captain general of western Cuba and the top Spanish authority on the island, and argued that her father was innocent and not responsible for his daughter's opinions. She could have stopped there, but that was not her style: "I, on the other hand," she added, "do not hide the fact that I detest [your] government, and that I will do anything in my power to help overthrow it."[5]

As the firmness of her language reveals, Casanova had a clear understanding of what rights modern citizenship entailed and would not settle for less. Her abrasiveness, while an effective political tool, was widely condemned. Poet Leopoldo Turla dedicated these lines of warning to her:

Tame your martial spirit, Emilia,
Do not pour your noble ardor into a bloody fight
Do not let the meek and shy dove
Turn into a war hawk.[6]

Writing in response, Emilia defended her intrusion into political affairs by arguing, as she often did, that men were incompetent:

> Military matters, I realize, are not a woman's business, but one would have to have no blood in one's veins not to be outraged to see the fatherland in danger and those in a position to help be either indifferent to the crisis or occupied with their own advancement, rather than with their country's salvation. When everything up until now has been mistakes or failures, it seems to me sometimes that, if we women took the initiative for the expeditions, at least we would take that responsibility from the inept hands they are now in and give that charge to men who are brave and determined patriots. If no trustworthy Cuban turns up on time, the League of Cuba's Daughters at this moment is gathering what is needed, guns, gunpowder, bullets, to dispatch an expedition, and to appoint among its members two or three to lead it.

She finished her letter by requesting that the poet send his photograph to be included in her album.[7]

The hostility Emilia Casanova encountered from members of the émigré community, and even from many of her political friends, stemmed in part from her uncompromising—and not always wise—political choices, which placed her at odds with her countrymen. The acerbic tone of the criticism, however, can be attributed to her being a woman who violated her society's definition of femininity. As a woman, Emilia was particularly vulnerable to the backbiting and gossip at clubs and *tertulias*, where it was said that she should keep busy with sewing, not politics. Some of those comments made their way into the progovernment Cuban press, which delighted in printing vicious caricatures and ugly insinuations about her public and private behavior. She complained:

> I was the first one to give my name and to encourage other women to do the same to begin this new crusade against the oppressor of my country. I was convinced that I would receive insults and affronts from the *españolería* (Spanish jingoists) in Cuba as reward for my services; but I was certainly not prepared to hear that some of my compatriots, who, having not shown that they will brandish the sword against the common enemy, are brandishing their tongue and pen against one of the few Cubans who has the honor of having deserved the hatred of the "volunteers" [a reference to mobs of Spaniards who burned her in effigy in Cárdenas and Matanzas].[8]

Emilia claimed to be unscathed by the criticism she received: "The accusations make no impression on me," she wrote in July, 1869, "they make me laugh."[9] But, naturally, she was not completely immune to her detractors. On December 28, 1869, she wrote again to Capt. Gen. Domingo Dulce, complaining about the vitriol the Spanish media directed toward her and other Cuban ladies: "It is not common among Cuban women to address captains general the way I am doing, but it has been a while since I emancipated myself from the colonial tutelage. And so I think I can exercise the right that all free people who come of age have to complain about their immediate superiors. It seems that, since you are accustomed to having 'Messalinas' as queens, you measure all of us by the same standards and that you do not expect modesty even from your own mothers, sisters, and wives." [Messalina, Roman emperor Claudio's wife, was known for her many lovers, as was Spanish queen Isabella II.] These were harsh words, she admitted, especially coming from a woman. But she had been driven to indignation by the orchestrated campaign of slander against her. She finished her letter by reiterating that her "resolution to shake the European yoke and achieve independence [was] far superior to any insults, lampoons, and atrocities that the malicious genius of the Spanish despotism may invent to stop me."[10]

Hurt or not, the criticism Emilia Casanova received did little to cool her political ardor and determination to promote the Cuban cause. She helped families who had left the island as victims of the government's repression. She collected and sent money for the rebel army. And she wrote letters seeking support from important world figures, such as Giuseppe Garibaldi. "We began our revolution," she wrote to the Italian leader, "freeing our own slaves, arming them and incorporating them into the patriotic ranks, and that is why, you will realize, our purpose is universal freedom."[11] He politely responded: "I have been from the beginning and with all my soul with your glorious revolution. I will always be with the oppressed, whether the oppressors are kings or nations."[12]

Emilia held up her commitment to the rebel cause as an example to other women. She advised a female collaborator:

Action and courage. If you could see my life since the revolution began, you would understand that I don't recommend one thing and do another one. I have breakfast at 7:00, then I run to New York and spend the day busy with patriotic activities. There are nine miles between my house and the city. I have to go to the station by carriage, take the train at 8:00 and the tram or omnibus at 9:00. I return home for dinner in the evening and follow the same routine the next day. So that the only time I have for my children is at night, not counting the large correspondence to which I must also attend.[13]

Emilia Casanova's most controversial action was the campaign she organized to discredit the secret peace negotiations in 1871 between the Spanish government and members of the New York junta. For many Cuban insurgents, on the island and abroad, discussing a cease-fire amounted to treason. Casanova mistrusted the government in exile, which was composed mainly of affluent Cubans. She argued that their commitment to the rebellion was tepid at best. Answering a question a friend had posed about Miguel Aldama, head of the junta and one of the wealthiest men in Cuba, she wrote: "You ask me who Aldama is, and I'll simply tell you he is not one of us. First, his fortune places him with the aristocracy of money. Second, his education, habits, and closeness to the Conservative Party, which he accepts, make him reject the revolution, since he is certain that with its triumph, the free and independent people, a democracy, will begin to govern Cuba."[14]

When the junta sent poet Juan Clemente Zenea to Cuba to negotiate a peace agreement between Spain and the rebels, Emilia Casanova mobilized the women of her network to condemn his mission. Anita Quesada, wife of Carlos Manuel Céspedes, president of the Cuban republic, attended one of the meetings of the League of Cuba's Daughters, where a resolution was passed chastising the negotiations. Her presence seemed to indicate Cespedes's agreement with Casanova's views; Aldama then resigned as head of the junta. Defending her action, Casanova made clear to Céspedes that her disagreement with the junta was not only tactical but also rooted in deep ideological differences: "It so happens that those who from the beginning took the reins of our country's public interests have always been in disagreement with me, and not only about the ways and means to carry the revolution to a happy ending. And no wonder we disagree: They have been concessionists, then reformists, then autonomists, while I have always been in favor of independence."[15]

The criticism directed at Emilia Casanova only intensified when Spain, after a change of government, decided that Zenea, who had fallen prisoner, was no longer a useful mediator and condemned him to death in order to satisfy the most intransigent Spanish sectors in Cuba. Having been so strongly opposed to Zenea's negotiations, Casanova was viewed more than ever as unfeeling and somehow responsible for the events that ended with the poet's demise.

She, however, persevered with her political agenda. Her next cause was to convince the U.S. Congress to grant belligerency status to the rebels, an action that the Cuban insurgency desperately needed in order to put an end to American support for Spain. [According to international law, belligerency status allows an insurgent force to enjoy a certain degree of political sovereignty, including diplomatic engagement with neutral states.] A letter Emilia Casanova wrote to her son while she was in Washington conveys how well versed she was in the politics of her time. She wanted her husband to help her craft the petition, but, in the letter to their son, she tells him exactly what she wants the petition to say:

> In order to convince the United States to grant belligerency rights, the petition should be based on the fact that the United States is responsible for the Cuban people's oppression, because it opposed Bolívar's liberation plans and because it has always helped Spain, today more than ever, even though the pretext for such aberration and contradiction—the fear that the abolition of slavery in Cuba would endanger the tranquillity of the southern states—is no longer justifiable.
>
> The petition should also argue that there will be slaves in our dear country as long as the Spanish occupy a piece of land in it; and that the ruin and desolation of that beautiful and very wealthy island will be certain and complete if the war continues. And that the wealth and prosperity of the island of Cuba are important to the commerce, navy, industry, and agriculture of this country and every state of the union.[16]

A few weeks later, Casanova presented her request to the U.S. Congress. She characterized the struggle against Spain as a war of independence and asked the United States to maintain "strict neutrality."[17] Her plea, however, went unanswered. Not until 1898, the year after she died, did the American government reverse its position and deem the rebels worthy of support.

In 1872, a group of women who had collaborated with Casanova broke away from the League of Cuba's Daughters and formed their own club. Like many other Cuban rebels, they felt that she was too controversial and too difficult to work with. But Emilia Casanova had a lasting impact on Cuban society that even her detractors could not dismiss. Her decisiveness opened new possibilities for women's activism in exile. The women's club would become the most effective instrument in the nationalist struggle in the 1890s, when women's participation reached the level of a true mass movement.[18]

It was inevitable that Casanova's unapologetic demand for the rights of citizenship would stir tensions within the insurgent forces. The rebel government never contemplated that an expansion of women's rights should be one of the results of this war. Similarly, it is not surprising that some of the women who fought against Spain would expect their participation to be translated into a bigger role in society.

No woman embodies the Mambisas' double aspirations for Cuba's freedom and women's citizenship better than Ana Betancourt. A writer, conspirator, ideologue, and feminist, she devoted all her energy to the rebel cause and, consequently, lost everything she loved. She was born in Puerto Príncipe in 1832, the same year as Ana Casanova, at "a time when all that most Camagüeyan ladies knew consisted of praying, at best, how to read their prayer book, and barely writing."[19]

In 1854, she married Ignacio Mora, also a Camagüeyan. Like many other young men of comfortable means, Mora studied in Havana and Spain. He later traveled throughout Europe during the turbulent 1840s, a decade of popular and nationalist uprisings. He finished his education in the United States, where he met Gaspar Betancourt Cisneros, "El Lugareño", the annexationist leader who was so influential among the Camagüeyan youth. Through him, Ignacio Mora entered annexationist circles, even helping finance some of their expeditions. By the time he returned home, Mora was a staunch supporter of democracy and a firm believer in the benefits of Cuba's annexation to the United States.

Ana Betancourt. Fondo Cubano, Betancourt, BNJM

From early in their marriage, Ignacio and Ana worked as a team. She helped him rebuild his family's fortune, which had been severely depleted by his failed revolutionary attempts. He helped her improve her writing and reading skills and encouraged her to learn French and English. Being a member of a family with firm ties to the opposition forces, Ana was not a stranger to the politics of the Cuban insurgency. However, she credited Ignacio for shaping her political views. In her *Memoirs*, Ana describes her husband in loving terms: "He was a handsome lad, friendly, honest, happy, and prodigiously generous. He was an intelligent youth who knew how to keep company. Humane with his slaves, he considered them members of his own family. He was happy because he was good, and he loved me deliriously, he came to make a paradise out of his home. With me he shared not only his material wealth, but also his intellectual knowledge. He taught me so much that our thoughts and feelings were one and the same."[20]

When the war began in 1868, their home became a meeting place for the rebels. She wrote revolutionary pamphlets and helped her husband edit and distribute the rebel paper *El Mambí*. "People deposited arms and war supplies in our home, which was where the emissaries coming from Bayamo, las Tunas, and Manzanillo stayed. I was in charge of writing and distributing proclamations among the people and the military."[21]

Soon afterward, her husband left Puerto Príncipe to join the fighting. The couple's parting words, as she recorded them, show how the rebels infused religious significance into their struggle for *la patria* and suggest how she longed to be part of that sacred cause:

At nine o'clock in the evening on the third day of November, 1869, my Ignacio said farewell. They were going to revolt the next day. "I have come to say goodbye to you," he told me, embracing me in his arms. "The time has come to throw ourselves into the fight: tomorrow we are going to rise and I come to say good-bye. Might I be chasing a ghost in my quest to free Cuba? Today I cannot decipher this enigma, but it is a religion and as with all religions it must have its martyrs. . . . Consider yourself a widow from now on, for this way the news of my death will be less painful."

"And with you dead," I asked him, "what shall I do alone on this earth? Unite me with your destiny, put me to work in some way, I, too, wish to consecrate my life to the homeland."[22]

After her husband left, Ana Betancourt continued her political involvement in Puerto Príncipe, as the sole editor of *El Mambí*. But by December, 1868, her situation had become too dangerous, and she joined Ignacio in the *manigua*.

In 1869, the First Constitutional Assembly convened in Guáimaro, the rebel capital. Ana Betancourt attended the meeting and asked to speak on behalf of the Cuban woman. Her words are among the first feminist speeches recorded in Latin American history: "Citizens: The Cuban woman in the dark and peaceful corner of the home waited patiently and resignedly for this beautiful hour, when a revolution would break her yoke and untie her wings. Citizens: Everything was enslaved in Cuba: cradle, color, and sex. You want to destroy the enslavement of the cradle, fighting until death. You have destroyed the slavery of color by emancipating the slave. The time has come to free women."[23]

The records indicate that Céspedes congratulated her, but it is hard to know how revolutionary leaders responded to Betancourt's words. It is likely that women's determined presence in the war, as well as the vibrant revolutionary spirit in the air, fostered a new degree of respect for women's status among the rebels even if, as we saw with Emilia Casanova, the line that separated heroic matronly behavior from improper unfeminine intrusion was easily crossed.

Ana Betancourt spent three years in rebel territory always defending the need to continue the armed struggle. Hearing of the compromise being discussed between the junta in New York and the Spanish government to end the war, she, like Emilia Casanova, objected. She wrote to her husband and his comrades: "My Ignacio: I hope that you all receive those peacemakers as they deserve. Tell them, as El Lugareño would say, that you are old and experienced dogs and won't fall into that trap. Tell them that the world is walking toward democracy and that it can have no other form than the American one, which encompasses political, moral, religious, and economic freedom."[24]

By the time the Ten Years War began, the American Civil War was over, and the American South no longer viewed slaveholding Cubans as possible allies. With the decrease of American support, people like Ignacio Mora, who saw their hopes for annexation evaporate, set their aspirations on the independence cause. But, as Betancourt's words of admonition indicate, the democratic ideals the northern neighbor embodied continued to inspire the Cuban rebels' actions.

As for Ana Betancourt, she was caught July 9, 1871, and taken to prison, where she almost died of typhoid fever. By the time she was released from jail, she had lost her hair and nearly her sanity. She then began her exile. She describes her arrival in New York as a "terrible day": "Young, almost without resources; not knowing where to direct myself and having no one waiting for me, I leaned over the rail of the ship and looked to see if there were any familiar persons among the countless gentlemen on the pier. Each passenger collected his luggage and left. I remained motionless, as though stupefied, not knowing what to do."[25]

One of her husband's fellow Masons came to the rescue and took her to a boardinghouse where other Cuban immigrants lived. While in the United States, she could at least communicate with Americans, thanks to the years she had spent studying English. She was luckier in that regard than most Cuban women.

Like Concha Agramonte, Amalia Simoní, and many other Cuban women in exile, Ana Betancourt now had to make a living. In New York, she went to work in a sweatshop. Describing the ordeal of the women who worked there, Aurelia Castillo writes: "The sound of the sewing machine, accelerated by the pedaling of the small foot, accompanied the happy songs with which mothers, daughters, and sisters sang to distract themselves from their misery and, mercifully, to try to fool each other. And when hunger and disease called at the gates of these lively workers, they lowered their heads before the decrees of destiny; but there was always a defiant gesture, a proud and dignified word to reject the dishonor if it dared to present itself among them."[26]

While in New York, Ana Betancourt received Ignacio's first letter since their separation: "My Good Anita: I am still ignorant of your fate, I know not of your destination nor of how you were treated by the enemy. What a terrible situation! Oh! The fatherland makes great demands, and the harshest of all is the near-death that is the eternal separation from your most beloved possessions."[27]

In New York, it did not take long for Emilia Casanova to recruit Ana Betancourt as a political agitator. The mixture of admiration and trepidation that Ana felt toward Emilia can be seen in her ambivalent response when Emilia asked her to come along to visit Ulysses S. Grant. This meeting was to request that the American government intercede on behalf of a group of first-year medical students in Havana who had been arrested for vandalizing a Spanish journalist's grave. Grant received the two women and indicated his willingness to help, but asked them not to let the object of their visit be known so as to avoid a diplomatic mishap. The official version made it sound like the women had asked the president to grant the Cuban rebels belligerency status, and that he had ignored their request. That two women would take upon themselves such an ambitious political task was considered laughable. "On my return to New York," Ana wrote, "I had to bear in silence the scolding and criticisms of my friends. Their admonishments were made even crueler by their assumption that Ignacio would be upset with me. I, who knew Ignacio and knew of his faith in my good judgment, paid no attention."[28] She was right. After Ignacio heard of his wife's political involvement, he wrote to her: "What a joy. Anita is in New York and working for Cuba. Oh! I'm happy!"[29]

When Emilia Casanova sent a note to the New York *Herald* announcing how several Cuban ladies had gone to the White House to ask that Cuba be granted belligerency status, Ana Betancourt was appalled. Later on she commented: "I found such audacity distasteful." Yet on the next line she acknowledges how important their mission was. Indeed, although seven of the students were executed, the rest had their sentence reduced to exile in Spain. Betancourt rejoiced: "When success crowned our venture and when it was known that the students had been removed from the jail and sent to Spain on account of our intervention, my critics were finally silenced. I will always be grateful to Emilia for having included me in such a saintly and merciful mission."[30]

On the advice of her brothers, Ana Betancourt moved to Jamaica, a cheaper place to live and closer to home. There she worked in a school teaching mostly Cuban girls. Ignacio was delighted: "I congratulate you for acquiring the glorious title of School Teacher. Good, Anita, very good. You have begun to gather the fruits of your beautiful intelligence."[31]

While in exile Ana learned that her two sisters-in-law and their children had been killed in the *manigua*. A similar fate awaited her husband. She was teaching in Jamaica when she learned the devastating news that Ignacio Mora had been taken prisoner and executed.

By the end of the Ten Years War, Ana Betancourt was a broken woman in soul and body. Ironically, she took refuge with her sister, who had married a Spanish army officer, and lived the rest of her life in Spain.[32]

By 1876, the rebellion had lost momentum. The Mambí army had been unable to penetrate the western part of the island and had lost control of former strongholds such as Camagüey. That did not mean the Spanish army had managed to overpower the rebels. In fact, despite having sent more soldiers to Cuba than to any other colony, the Spanish government could not proclaim victory. Using guerrilla warfare as its strategy, and with the support of the population, the rebel army was hard to defeat. Malaria, dysentery, and other tropical diseases also did their part in decimating the Spanish army.

This long, cruel war had cost thousands of lives, and the countryside had been devastated. With no clear winner and no end in sight, during the last two years of the war, the rebels began to talk about the need for a political compromise. The long conflict had brought few results and great frustration. Besides, the rebels were not a unified lot. Some complained that the Mambí leadership had become too radical; some feared that the leadership was too heavily dominated by blacks. Consequently, many rebels turned to more moderate options such as autonomy and reform.

Taking advantage of the tensions within the rebel camp, Spain issued the conditions for a resolution to the war. In 1877, the government promised that rebels who put down their weapons would be pardoned without reprisals. The majority, though not all, of the rebel forces accepted Spain's conditions and in 1878 got ready to sign the Pact of Zanjón. The Ten Years War was over, but the ideals that drove Cubans by the thousands to fight against Spain remained merely dormant.

6

▲▼▲▼▲

"It Won't Be Long"

Between the Wars

The Pact of Zanjón put an end to the Ten Years War, yet not all insurgent soldiers willingly abandoned their weapons. Particularly in Oriente, rebels resisted accepting a peace that failed to meet demands they considered nonnegotiable, such as the abolition of slavery. The Maceo brothers, Guillermo Moncada, and other officers from the eastern part of the island, many of them of African descent, stated their opposition to the pact's conditions in a document known as the Baraguá Protest. Supported by about four thousand soldiers, they took up arms again in the summer of 1879, in what is called, for its brevity—a mere nine months—the Guerra Chiquita (the Little War).

After the Spanish army crushed this uprising, the fighters faced the hard reality of exile. Some had been preceded by their families. At the end of the Ten Years War, Antonio Maceo's relatives–his mother, Mariana Grajales; his wife, María Cabrales; and his sisters—had come down from the mountains and been shipped off to Jamaica. But those who went into exile after losing the Guerra Chiquita faced greater risks when captured. In 1880, a group of fighters and their families, including the Moncada clan, left Oriente for Jamaica. Before they could arrive at the neighboring island, they were intercepted by Spanish soldiers, who sent the men to jail in Spain and took the women and children back to Cuba, except the five Moncada women who, with their children, were left in a rowboat between Jamaica and Cuba. Dominga Moncada, Guillermo's mother, already in her seventies, acted as the main rower on this long trip back to Cuba.

We can only speculate about whether the Moncadas were singled out because Guillermo was such a prominent warrior or because of Dominga's well-known antipathy to the government, or if they were punished for the color of their skin. Dominga saw her son Guillermo taken to jail in Mahón, Spain, where he contracted tuberculosis. Francisca, Guillermo's eighteen-year-old daughter, was also sent to jail in Spain as punishment for her father's militancy. They were not able to return to Cuba until 1886.[1]

Like the Moncadas and the Maceos, in the aftermath of the war, many Mambí families migrated to places such as Costa Rica, El Salvador, Mexico, Jamaica, New York, and Florida. A foreign environment, at times, a new language, and, worst of all, the memories of so many loved ones who had died for what remained an unfulfilled ideal made exile a bitter experience. Poor and lonely, they relied on each other for survival. Military leader Máximo Gómez, in exile in Jamaica, wrote in his diary: "Things are still going poorly, my resources are exhausted, and I don't know how to feed my children. I went out to sell an old coat, I could not sell it. My wife then sent a blanket over to María, Maceo's wife, and she bought it for five pesos." Those five pesos were all the Gómez family would have until the end of the month.[2]

The duration of exile varied widely. While some families were able to go back after a few months, others had to wait years, and for some, exile was their final destination. Many, however, continued to play an active role in politics.

After the Ten Years War, Cuban residents in New York, in support of the rebels who challenged the Pact of Zanjón, formed the Cuban Revolutionary Committee (Comité Revolucionario Cubano), which encouraged the founding of nationalist clubs to promote the island's independence. Women were asked to participate. In October of 1878, the committee invoked the names of independence leaders throughout the American continent and issued this call: "Ladies who sympathize with the cause of Cuban independence: Cuban women! We count on you to help us disinfect our country from the Iberian epidemic that is destroying it. American women! Don't forget that the work initiated by Bolívar, Washington, Sucre, San Martín, Hidalgo, O'Higgins, and other champions of our independence will not be finished until we tear the Iberian flag from its last possessions in this continent: Cuba and Puerto Rico."[3]

Liberty's Daughters clubs were organized in locations where a cluster of women was willing to work for Cuba's independence. Club members filled the positions of president, treasurer, and secretary by election, and these groups then formalized their ties with the Cuban Revolutionary Committee in New York. However, the nationalist cause suffered a serious blow with the insurgents' defeat in the Guerra Chiquita, and the women's organizations were inactive throughout the 1880s. Their power was again felt in the 1890s, when female networks fully bloomed.

Meantime, on the island, Cubans came to grips with the enormous losses the military conflict had wreaked. For the generation that was too young to have fought, especially the urban youth of the western provinces, who had heard only secondhand accounts, this was also a time to develop their own understanding of the events.

War veterans, now free to interact with the civilian population and to express their views, were able to tell their stories and reshape the way society perceived their role in the conflict. Many Cubans came to view these veterans with great admiration, as heroic Davids competing against a well-equipped and evil Goliath. Despite their obvious military inferiority, the Cuban fighters had kept the colonial army at bay for ten long years, and if they had not been able to defeat Spain, they had not been crushed by it either. Surrounded by the warrior's mystique, the former rebel became a charismatic figure: "The city youth shook hands with the men whose faces had been tanned by the sun of the plains and the gunpowder of combat and fought for the honor of meeting them. The ladies felt proud to be seen accompanied by one of those seasoned men who, during the best years of their lives, had sustained the solemn pact they made with death in order to achieve universal freedom for Cuba."[4]

Although no longer defended on the battlefield, Cuban nationalism continued to be addressed in civil society. In the 1880s and the early 1890s, the island's population explored with gusto what it meant to be Cuban as opposed to Spanish. And women, who in the postwar years had increasing access to secondary and higher education, joined this debate. In *tertulias* and parties, banquets and literary gatherings, Cubans favored cultural manifestations with a distinct Creole flavor. In Martín Morúa Delgado's novel *Sofía*, written in these postwar years, a young woman at a party chooses to play a light piece on the piano by an anonymous Cuban composer. One woman rebukes her, saying, "She's playing those Cuban melodies again! . . . You call that music?" But the other guests truly appreciate the Cuban song, one of them emphasizing the importance of popular music.[5] Proof of Creole culture's vitality in the postwar years is found in the birth of the *danzón*, a fusion of African and Spanish rhythms, of court and country movements, that would soon become the national dance. It was during this period, too, that a characteristic version of Cuban religious practices emerged, as both African and Catholic beliefs influenced each other and competed for the island's heart and soul.[6]

In an insightful study on the impact of the Lucumí religion in Cuba, Miguel W. Ramos discusses the crucial role women played in the survival and transmission of African-based religions. He argues that three priestesses from western Africa were instrumental in shaping the religious practices that came to dominate the island. For Afro-Cubans, religion was one of the few connections they had to their past, a source of identity and pride. The women's influence revitalized the meaning of the forgotten rituals, helped unify different ethnic groups, and gave the former slaves a platform from which to negotiate their permanent position on the island.[7]

The devotion to African deities could be maintained only by merging their worship with the Catholic faith. The revered figure of Our Lady of Charity, the patron saint of Cuba, for instance, found a syncretistic correspondence in Oshun, goddess of love and fertility, and inspired fighters in both capacities. This fusion of religious traditions that developed in Cuba in the mid-1800s became an increasingly important aspect of national identity, even though the rebel rhetoric failed to acknowledge the power of the African-based religious practices among its ranks and supporters.

Culture and nationalism met at the home of the Borrero family, whose *tertulias* in the 1880s and the early 1890s were attended by writers, poets, and literary critics, many of them veterans of the Ten Years War. Poetry, philosophy, music, new scientific discoveries, and, of course, politics, were among the subjects that the members of this circle debated. Esteban Borrero, accompanied by his five outspoken daughters, presided over the meetings. One of them, Juana Borrero, merely a teenager, contributed to the meetings with readings of sensual poems and patriotic verses that encouraged Cubans to go back to the battlefield and fight for freedom. She asked in one of her poems whether the sacrifice of so many Cubans in the previous war would be in vain: "It's not possible! Wait! It won't be long/'til the yearned cry of freedom/among the confused clamor of battle/shakes your sacred remains."[8]

Aurelia Castillo also pondered with frustration Cubans' inactivity. After a long stay in Europe and America with her Spanish husband, she returned home to find what she thought was a morally and physically devastated society. In her 1890 piece "De regreso" [Upon returning], she compares the progress she witnessed in some European countries with the apathy and backwardness of Cuba that resulted from Spain's control over the island's affairs. With a brav-

Juana Borrero. Fondo Cubano, Borrero, BNJM

ery that would lead to her expulsion from Cuba a few years later, she accused the colonial government of having brought all sorts of ills to the island, from slavery to corruption to despotism to inefficiency. But her goal was not so much to denounce Spain's role in Cuba as to encourage other Cubans to take responsibility for the state of their society. Asking them to think of themselves as adults who needed no tutelage, hers was a call for political and psychological independence from the metropolis.[9]

Changes were not occurring fast enough in the political sphere to satisfy the nationalist longing for an independent identity, but the postwar years in fact saw a great transformation in Cuba's social fabric. During this period, thousands of Cuban slaves were gradually freed from bondage. One of the conditions the rebels had won in the Pact of Zanjón was the release of slaves who fought in the insurgent army. Although Spain had refused to abolish slavery, it could not keep some slaves in chains while freeing the ones who participated in the rebellion. An 1880 ruling abolished slavery in Cuba, but left the slaves under their masters' "protectorate." In 1886, the *patrocinados*, or "protected" slaves, were finally granted freedom, bringing the institution of slavery to an end on the island.

Emancipation gave former slaves a reason to feel invested in the national project. It also made it imperative for them to find a means of subsistence. Many former slaves found staying on the plantation unpalatable and drifted to the cities, where they competed for the few jobs available to unskilled workers, their job search further limited by racial discrimination. In other emancipated families, the men continued to do agricultural work as hired laborers while their wives found employment as maids, cooks, and laundresses in the nearest town. At harvest time, when the wages were higher, the women often went back to work in the fields.[10] Rebecca Scott points out how women working outside their communities helped diminish the isolation of rural life. Going back and forth from one environment to the other, the women brought information and new ideas to their families. They also helped maintain awareness in town of what was happening in the countryside.[11]

The more urbane, educated blacks developed their own platforms from which to examine society. As Carmen Montejo Arrechea has written, in 1888, a new magazine, *Minerva*, was established to target black women. The bimonthly publication promoted self-esteem and education among its readers and contrasted the lack of opportunities black women had in Cuba with the improving conditions of their sisters in the United States. From its pages, writers both denounced the racial and sexual oppression that women of color still endured after slavery and defended the ideals of a free Cuba, which had not yet been realized.[12]

Despite cautionary warnings like the ones in the pages of *Minerva*, the 1880s were a time of political optimism. The Spanish government's renewed promises to grant greater political rights to the island's inhabitants led some sectors to support an "autonomist" solution: many came to believe that the answer to the island's ills was to maintain the colonial connection while asking for reforms and a high degree of freedom and autonomy. There remained, however, strong voices that warned against trusting Spain's vague offers and that continued to agitate for independence, a dangerous activity that, if discovered, could result in imprisonment. A young writer from Havana, José Martí, was deported to Spain for opposing Spanish rule. Martí, however, managed to escape and make his way to New York, where he became the guiding force of Cuba's independence.

In 1892 in Florida, José Martí founded the Partido Revolucionario Cubano (PRC; Cuban Revolutionary Party) with the goal of overthrowing the colonial government. In addition to creating a party structure tight and secretive enough to withstand Spain's repression, Martí, drawing on the tradi-

María Cabrales. Fondo Cubano, Cabrales. Sobre 7, BNJM

tion of revolutionary clubs, inspired the reemergence of a grassroots movement in which the average Cuban—male or female—could participate. Martí
understood how important it was to have women on the side of the rebellion,
and he promoted the founding of women's clubs as a patriotic duty. Once
again, female virtue was the best proof of the cause's worthiness: "The people's
campaigns are weak only when women offer them merely fearful and re-
strained assistance; when the woman of timid and quiet nature becomes ex-
cited and applauds, when the cultured and virtuous woman anoints the work
with the sweet honey of her affection—the work is invincible."[13]

María Cabrales, Antonio Maceo's wife, responded to Martí's call. She was
born in San Luis in 1842, and, like her husband, belonged to a family of free
mulattoes from the east. Although her mother-in-law, Mariana Grajales, was
illiterate, Cabrales read and wrote with ease. She spent the Ten Years War in the
manigua, moving from one rebel camp to another. After losing her two small
children, she became a devoted nurse to the insurgent soldiers, who marveled
at her willingness to climb the toughest terrain and her solicitousness when
caring for the sick.[14] One fighter recounted how, during the war, when the rebel
forces found themselves weakening and the suggestion was made that the
women leave because they could not be protected, Cabrales complained: "And
if there are no longer women, who will nurse the wounded?"[15]

Hermanas de Maceo Club. Fondo Cubano, Cabrales. Sobre 8, BNJM

As much as she could, she stayed with her husband, taking care of him the many times he was hurt. After the war, María Cabrales went on a pilgrimage from one place of exile to another: Jamaica, Haiti, Saint Domingue, Honduras, Panama, and the United States. In May, 1893, she and her husband met in Costa Rica after a separation of more than two years. Her husband's extramarital affairs were heartbreaking, particularly the news, in April, 1881, that Maceo had fathered a son with another woman.[16]

But Cabrales continued to play a role in Cuban politics. In 1892, while still in Jamaica, she founded and headed the José Martí women's club (Club de Mujeres José Martí). This was mostly a black women's group. The color line, even if challenged explicitly by revolutionary rhetoric and ignored often by military men, could not be erased overnight. Yet for prominent political figures like Maceo or Cabrales, crossing the race line was not impossible. Later, in Costa Rica, where she spent most of her years in exile, Cabrales organized the Cuban women's club of Costa Rica (El Club de las Mujeres Cubanas de Costa Rica), later known as Sisters of María Maceo (Hermanas de María Maceo), a racially mixed group that raised funds for the rebel army.

Martí was pleased. María Cabrales's initiative would encourage other women to organize similar groups. After visiting the Maceos in Costa Rica in 1893,

Martí invoked María's name, just as he did that of her mother-in-law, Mariana Grajales, as a symbol of bravery and commitment to the Cuban cause: "María, the woman, the very noble lady, who is afraid of nothing—not even death, because she has seen its shadow so many times . . . Ah, easy it is to be a hero with such women!"[17]

During the Ten Years War, the New York junta had relied on the support of conservative and affluent landowners. By the 1890s, under Martí's influence, the working-class émigré community was asked to play a prominent role. A phenomenally prolific writer and powerful speaker, Martí expressed the need for all races and social classes to participate in creating the new Cuba. His views, however, were not shared by all. Tension between the wealthier, conservative classes and the more militant workers resulted in constant friction.

Equally explosive at times was the coexistence of black and white nationalists. In fact, white Cubans were concerned to see so many black men rise to the highest ranks of the rebel army. The Spanish government, with the support of the wealthiest landowners, exploited this fear, warning white Cubans that officers such as Antonio Maceo were engaged not in a struggle to free Cuba but in a race war against whites.[18] These insinuations had their intended effect. The Cuban government in exile slighted Maceo, the most capable military figure that the Cuban army had, in favor of lesser figures, to avoid controversy. "Antes españoles que africanos" [Spanish rather than African] became the rallying cry of the Cuban upper classes.

These racist positions were shared by a number of Cuban exiles, including those the Cuban army counted on for financial support and some of whom subsequently withdrew their aid. Martí turned then to the tobacco workers of Florida for financial assistance, arguing that it was not the wealthy Cubans who best represented the island's interests, but the poor and hard-working patriots whose generosity and sacrifice for the Cuban cause were truly meaningful. The workers' economic contribution was not substantial.[19] Yet the working-class support for the cause of independence gave the struggle a democratic, popular dimension absent in the Ten Years War.

In the 1880s, a vibrant émigré community flourished in Florida. The economic crisis of this decade had forced some 100,000 Cubans to seek employment in the tobacco factories of Key West and Tampa, where the cigar industry had relocated. With a firm working-class consciousness and militant spirit, the tobacco workers emerged as a cohesive and savvy group that was familiar with books, writers, and ideas that questioned the established order. In their factories, Cuban workers discussed Karl Marx's attack on capitalism, Charles

Dickens's reflections on the Industrial Revolution, and the views of Russian and Spanish anarchists. It is hard to determine how aware women were of these discussions, but it is clear they had a presence in the tobacco industry work force. After the Ten Years War, many cigar factories, first on the island then later in Florida, began to offer women jobs for lower wages than men's.[20] By the mid-1890s, 9 percent of the tobacco workers in Florida were women.[21] As workers, women attended meetings, discussed financial matters, and voted on whether to support strikes, activities that would prove useful to the nationalist cause.[22] Carolina Rodríguez was one of them.

Carolina "the Patriot" Rodríguez was born in Santa Clara and actively opposed the colonial government in the Ten Years War. Like many other Cubans, economic necessity in the 1880s forced her into exile in Florida, where she found a job making dismal wages as a *despalilladora,* a stripper of tobacco leaves. Poor and almost blind, she was known among the émigré community for her enthusiastic and generous commitment to Cuba's independence. Martí chose to elevate this woman, his friend, as he had done with Mariana Grajales, to the stature of symbol of the Cuban nation:

> In the cold morning, old Carolina, wrapped up in her large shawl, goes out into the streets with the first laborers and takes the path to her workshop. She climbs the little set of stairs in the entryway and sits down, until it gets dark, at the table where she works. And when she collects on the unhappy week—since her hands, seventy years of age, can no longer do much work—she puts a few pesos in an envelope for another Cuban, one who is sick in Ceuta, in another envelope she puts some pesos for the Cubans they have wrongly jailed in Cuba. In the envelope she has left go two more pesos, and she sends them to the Cubanacán Club, because the president of this club seems like a real good Cuban to her and because Cubanacán is also the name she took in wartime. With the eyes of a sentry and the heart of a mother, the seventy-year-old woman guarantees freedom; she predicts the actions of her enemies; she knows where the suffering Cubans are—she goes to work for them, in the cold morning, wrapped in her wool cloak. That is the soul of Cuba![23]

Martí's affection for Carolina Rodríguez was reciprocated. Despite her precarious writing skills, she wrote to his collaborators in New York to demand that they protect their leader, "whom I love so much and though I'm strong I feel bad and nervous I want to see him outside that vipers' nest where there are so many cloven-hoofed beasts."[24] One of Carolina Rodríguez's fears was that the Spanish government would try to kill Martí. She wrote to Martí's secretary: "A Spaniard told a Cuban woman when Martí was sick that we should be careful because the Spanish government has given a large sum to have him poisoned and that there were poisons that let the person who had taken them live five or six months yesterday she told me and now in turn I'm telling you so that you all who have good doctors examine him to see if a remedy can be found to avoid this tragedy."[25]

Although Carolina Rodríguez's medical knowledge was vague, her fears of the danger Martí faced were well founded. There was evidence that Martí was the target of an assassination attempt during a trip to Tampa. His glass of wine was found to contain poison. Another tobacco worker, Paulina Pedroso, insisted after this that Martí stay at her home so that she could watch over him.

Paulina Pedroso was a *despalilladora* whose boardinghouse was a center of political activism. Paulina and her husband, Ruperto, political comrades and coconspirators, adored Martí. At their home, the PRC leader was pampered and treated like a son. With Martí's encouragement, the Pedrosos were active in La Liga de Instrucción de Tampa (Tampa's Instruction League), an educational center for black Cubans that promoted the ideals of the independence movement. Paulina often accompanied Martí on his fund-raising efforts to the tobacco factories. Once, when the workers seemed reluctant to make a contribution, Paulina, climbing to the podium, to Martí's amusement and delight, shamed the men by asking them to trade her dress for their pants.[26]

Paulina and Ruperto's commitment to the nationalist cause was so strong that once the War of Independence broke out they sold their home and gave the proceeds to the PRC in order to support the military effort. Although the contributions of most members of the émigré community seldom reached this magnitude, by the early 1890s there was a wealth of initiatives, many of them spurred by women's clubs, to help finance the fight against Spain.

In 1893, before the war began, women's clubs existed throughout the Cuban diaspora. Women's revolutionary groups flourished in Honduras, Costa Rica, Venezuela, El Salvador, Mexico, New York, and, of course, Florida. Mercedes Varona Club of New York, Hijas de la Libertad (Freedom's Daughters) in Key West, Hijas de la Patria (Fatherland's Daughters) in Ocala, and Obreras de la Independencia (Women Workers for Independence) in Tampa were among the women's groups already active in the years leading to the War of Independence. They formalized their goals in writing. For example, article no. 1 of the rules and regulations of the Sociedad Política Cubana Hijas de Hatuey (Cuban Political Club Daughters of Hatuey), founded in Saint Domingue in July, 1893, states that the club's exclusive goal is "to work for the absolute independence of the island of Cuba." Article no. 2 states that the group is open to "all *señoras o señoritas*, of any nationality, as long as they sympathize with the cause of Cuban independence and want to work for this goal." New members had to be sponsored by current ones and had to have the majority's approval.[27]

By the mid-1890s, Cuba and its expatriate community, both men and women, were ready to launch a new crusade for Cuban independence. In the spring of 1893, Spain, sensing that conflict in Cuba was about to erupt again, dispatched a member of the royal family, Princess Eulalia of Bourbon, to visit the island. Eulalia, twenty-eight years old and the youngest daughter of Queen Isabella II, became the first member of the Spanish royal family to visit the New World. Her mission was to pacify the island's increasing discontent and send the Cuban people the message that the Crown was interested in addressing their concerns. Writing to her mother, the princess recorded on May 8, 1893, the day of her arrival: "We have made a triumphant entrance here. The fears that some had with regards to the reception that was reserved for us in this, the capital of the island of Cuba, were indeed unfounded; their pessimism has been contradicted by reality."[28]

A few days later, however, Eulalia's optimism had evaporated, and she dutifully informed her mother of her changing views: "Every time that I touch

Princess Eulalia of Bourbon, Havana, 1893. Fondo Cubano, Eulalia, BNJM

lightly upon a colonial question, from everywhere I hear nothing but bitter complaints, and to the efforts I make in order to win over public opinion the response is always that Spain has abandoned Cuba for too long and should have been concerned about the island a long time ago."[29] A few days later she reported: "I have taken the opportunity afforded me by a party to study the sentiments that the aristocracy nourish toward Spain; there, like everywhere, I have found a sentiment that lets us foresee that on the day Cuba breaks off from the kingdom there will be a general relief for everyone."[30]

Despite the stormy horizons, Eulalia tried to do her bit to rally support for the Crown among the women she encountered. In her May 14 letter to her mother, she writes: "The women play a very important political role here. I have taken advantage of these circumstances, being that people from all the parties had been brought together, to draw up a message [of adherence] directed to the Queen Regent, that the ladies might sign it with me."[31]

It is no big surprise that the young princess's journey failed to achieve its mission. Within two years, Cuba was once again engulfed in a painful war, this time reaching a much larger segment of the population.

The period after the Ten Years War was a time for Cubans to reflect on the past and to ponder the future. Throughout civil society, cultural, religious, and social practices gave new meaning to what it meant to be Cuban. These were years of great social transformation. Emancipation freed the slaves, who now scrambled as best they could to make an autonomous living. The economic crisis of the 1880s forced thousands of Cubans to move to Florida, where they filled the ranks of a militant labor movement with a strong nationalist component. In exile, women entered the tobacco work force and joined pro-independence associations. In short, Cubans prepared to continue the fight.

7

▲▼▲▼▲

The War of Independence
(1895–1898)

In 1895, Cuban rebels once again declared war on Spain. This time the insurgents were equipped with clearly defined nationalist goals and a populist vision of the inclusive new society they wanted to create. Military men like Antonio Maceo and Máximo Gómez, who had lived in exile for more than a decade, returned to the island to lead the rebel forces. Also joining the insurgency was José Martí, who was killed in battle soon after his arrival. Despite his untimely death, Martí's commitment to Cuban independence inspired his compatriots for years to come.

When the war began in 1895, some of the old fighters were dead. Others remained in exile for political or family reasons. Many men and women who had been active in the Ten Years War, however, resumed their opposition to Spain, this time joined by a generation that had been too young to fight in the previous conflict.

Enrique Hernández Miyares celebrated women's continuing political involvement and their fierce determination to defend the Cuban cause, despite the passing of years and loved ones. Evoking the traditional role assigned to women in military conflicts, that is, reminding men of their duty to fight, Hernández Miyares claimed that the desire for revenge made Mambisas more eager to render service. They were waiting for their grandchildren to grow up

Mambisa with a rebel flag. Fondo Cubano, Grupos de Mambises, BNJM

so that, once again, they could send soldiers into battle. His poem "Eternal Needlewoman" (1897) reads as follows:

I
When the scream was heard in Yara
Her husband went to fight
Abandoning his home,
Hatred written on his face.
She, young as she was,
Filled with saintly enthusiasm,
Embroidered a glorious flag—
And wrapped in it would return,
Dead! Him whom she had loved so dearly.
II
Her son inherited a ferocious
Eagerness for redemption;
With fervent passion,

She embroidered another flag.
A flag that would become a shroud
For that expeditionary
Who, unfurling it in the air,
Died, a voluntary martyr,
In a Baire wasteland!
III
In the once-sweet home,
The widow instills respect.
As she brings up her grandchild
To know of vengeance!
The child grows and she hopes
That God hears her prayer—
To see him triumph, or that he die!
And meanwhile she embroiders another flag
With its solitary star.[1]

But women's participation in the War of Independence was more than embroidering flags and dreaming of revenge. It involved a wide array of clandestine activities that placed them at the political epicenter of the insurgency. As in the Ten Years War, some of these women were unwilling participants; they were simply caught in the conflict as wives, mothers, and daughters of rebel soldiers. Others were fully committed to the cause of independence. In both cases, the struggle against the colonial power tended to radicalize women, turning them into rebellious protagonists and giving those with a penchant for excitement a venue in which to satisfy it. Once again, they were needed allies.

Some women, like Concha Agramonte, were already grandmothers with a great deal of experience behind them when they resumed their political activity. Agramonte joined the rebel forces as soon as the war began and became Camagüey's agent for the Cuban government in exile. Others, like the Bolaño sisters, Rosario ("Violeta") and her sister Isabel ("Azucena"), were young and inexperienced. Both in their twenties, they sewed clothes for the army, nursed the wounded, cooked for the soldiers, and, most significantly, worked as emissaries and secret agents. In retaliation, their property was destroyed, forcing them to move to Havana, where they turned their home into a place for rebels to conspire, rest, and hide money.[2]

At the urging of the Cuban Revolutionary Party, and following the example set by María Cabrales, women of all classes and racial backgrounds, both on the island and in exile, enlisted in patriotic clubs. The Clemencia Báez Ladies' Club (Club de Damas Clemencia Baez), in Saint Domingue, is a good example of the goals and expectations of Cuban women's associations. As stated in its rules, the club's only objective was Cuba's independence. It was open to all women as long as they loved "the cause of Cuba's redemption" and wanted to contribute to this effort. The monthly fees were twenty-five cents, and the proceeds of fund-raising activities were to go entirely to the accounts of the New York junta. Club members were to meet regularly once a month and more often if the group's president deemed it necessary.[3]

By 1895, Key West was home to more than eighty clubs, twelve of them, at least, run by women. Tampa boasted more than thirty active women's clubs. On November 24, 1895, Ana Merchán founded in Tampa the Martí's Women Club (Discípulas de Martí). Soon more than eighty women had joined this group, devoting their energy to fund-raising and to "lifting the patriotic spirit." They organized bazaars, festivals, and parties. They visited store owners and businessmen and encouraged them to make generous contributions to the cause of independence.

Fredesvinda Sánchez and her sister Luisa founded the Castillo Duany Club (Club Castillo Duany). One of their activities was to procure cloth to make uniforms for the soldiers.[4] The women of Tampa's Justo Carrillo Club (Club Justo Carrillo) published *La Revista de Cuba Libre* and gave the paper's profits to the PRC. Similar activities kept other Cuban women in Florida and elsewhere busy. Even young Cuban girls formed clubs—The Two Flags (Las Dos Banderas) in New York and Cuban and Puerto Rican Girls (Niñas Cubanas y Portorriqueñas) and Cuba's Future Club (Club del Porvenir de Cuba) in Key West.

Women's clubs were named after Cuban patriots—for example, Flor Crombet Ladies Club (Club de Señoras Flor Crombet), after a general; Mariana Grajales Club (Club Mariana Grajales), after the prominent Ten Years War Mambisa—or invoked the political ideals, such as liberty and independence, of the nationalist movement.[5] Also popular were names such as Daughters of . . . and Disciples of . . . , revealing, as Paul Estrade has pointed out, the subordinate position that women, despite their activism, continued to assume in relation to men.[6]

Nationalist club members enjoyed having their picture taken, and these photographs are at times the only clue we have to the members' racial background. Blurry photographs of serious, proper-looking women tell us that in Tampa, for instance, the members of the Mercedes Varona No. 2 Club were black, the Mariana Grajales Club was integrated, and the Emilio Núñez Club had an all-white composition.

The War of Independence reduced the significance of race in defining one's identity and stressed the unity of all Cubans under one flag. Nationalism became a cause to be rallied around, regardless of race, and patriotic clubs were crucial in promoting racial integration. At their best, the clubs developed into embryonic democratic units where not only racial but also social and gender differences could be bridged. Nancy Hewitt describes how Mercedes Dueñas, from Tampa, founded the Lone Star Club (Estrella Solitaria Club). The group "became a meeting place where professionals, workers, whites, blacks, men and women could mingle."[7]

It was easier to be politically involved and join a patriotic group abroad than on the island, where the clubs remained illegal. But women in Cuba joined them by the thousands, nonetheless, and founded new groups or revived old ones that were active during the Ten Years War. Members were again sworn to secrecy and given a nom de guerre to be used when involved in revolutionary activity.

In 1895 in Cienfuegos, Rita Suárez, also known as "La Cubanita" and daughter of a rebel doctor, founded the first clandestine club for females on the island to become active in the War of Independence. Eleven women joined and two men were named honorary presidents. The group's activities included sewing bandages for wounded soldiers, making clothes out of flour sacks, preparing shipments of medicines and ammunition, and entering rebel territory with news and mail. Members were also charged with bringing information from the rebels to ships docked in the Cienfuegos harbor on their way to the United States, so that this information could reach the New York junta.[8]

In a letter dated October, 1897, an unidentified soldier who signed himself "Cienfuegos" wrote to Rita Suárez asking her to get him quinine, clothes, a tent, shoes, woolen shirts, a hat, and iodine. He finishes his note with a compliment that she must have appreciated: "I believe that your patriotic merits are greater than those of anyone I have known."[9]

As in exile, some clubs had a mixed membership of men and women, but most did not. In some cases, a group would have two branches, one for men and one for women, like Villa Clara's Juan Bruno Zayas and Bruno Zayas Sisters (Hermanas de Juan Bruno Zayas) clubs. Their new political role forced women to become highly resourceful. A group of Camagüeyan women, Aurelia Castillo recalled years later, thought of a plan to send secret information to other parts of the island. One of them traveled to Havana carrying her parakeet. The bars of the bird's cage were hollow and hid important documents for the delegates of the New York junta.[10] Victoria Caturla described how in 1897, the ladies in the rebel club of Remedios, her hometown in the province of Las Villas, were daring enough to steal arms at night from the Spanish soldiers who were sleeping in the main square. The women's ample skirts hid the weapons, which were tied to their legs or hung from their petticoats.[11]

The military conflict disrupted regular living patterns. As in the Ten Years War, at times, women found themselves without the usual protection of parents, husbands, or other relatives. Soldiers and civilians were subject to the war's unpredictable turns, which often sent them far from home and the familiar. Once again, the revolutionary government attempted to address moral standards. In September, 1896, the First Constitutional Assembly of Jimaguayú approved a new civil marriage law, which was to be accepted as a binding contract by all those who shared the revolutionary ideals. The unions were presided over by *prefectos*, acting in their role as municipal judges. Many of them, however, were illiterate, a fact that was later used to question the validity of the revolutionary marriages, thereby requiring those vows be renewed. This gave some men an opportunity to disclaim any commitment, which humiliated the women with whom they had exchanged vows during the war. "The Cuban woman marched to her marriage with full conviction and confidence that she was engaging in a public and legitimate act, believing in the authority and competence of the official who married her, and trusting the honor and patriotism of the man who was to become her husband," wrote Manuel Secades, who in 1902 denounced how often women were abandoned by their "war husbands."[12]

In other cases, both men and women ignored the legal tie contracted during the conflict and found new partners. Jesús Castellanos's war novel, *La manigua sentimental*, presents a scenario that seems nothing but plausible. The main character, a young rebel soldier, marries in the *manigua* under pressure from relatives and superiors. The couple is separated during an enemy attack and, eventually, dismissing the vows made during the conflict, they both marry other people.[13]

The rebel army also had strict policies against rape. On December 13, 1895, while Maceo and Gómez were getting ready for their western campaign, a war council condemned a soldier to be hanged for having committed rape.[14] But between rape and marriage lay a vast landscape of unregulated sexual behavior. Officers enjoyed the presence of lovers, usually poor young women who lived with them in the camps while their wives stayed in safer abodes.

When the War of Independence began in 1895, María Cabrales tried to go back to Cuba so that she could, once again, help the rebels. Her husband, Antonio Maceo, however, insisted that she stay in Costa Rica, arguing that she would be more useful to the insurgency from outside the island. Reluctantly, she had to accept. Perhaps his motivation to keep his wife away was not strictly political, since he was often involved with other women, yet Maceo definitely relied on her to act as a spokesperson for the Revolution. He regularly sent her information about the course of the war with the charge that she transmit his news to the media. Writing to his wife from the battlefield, Maceo's letters are full of patriotic rhetoric: "Fatherland above all else; your entire life is the best example; to continue means meeting our obligations, moving backward, shame with no honor. Onward, then; let us have the glory of sacrificing everything for the fatherland."[15] But the letters also reveal Maceo's practical interest in keeping María Cabrales informed of what was happening on the battlefield. During the April, 1895, campaign, he wrote: "I will try to write of the Revolution, so that you are able to keep the press up to date on what's happening in the countryside: I have six thousand men, well-armed and with ammunition. Much territory is already ours. On the fifteenth day of the coming month, I will have twelve thousand armed men and more territory conquered. Not a day goes by without my recruiting people. All the youths of Santiago de Cuba are leaving for the countryside. We have doctors and lawyers among us."[16] Describing to his wife the Spanish government's attempts to use women to get information about their enemies, Maceo explains: "[The Spaniards] use all available means. They've already started sending women to camps on the pretext that they're supposedly going to see their relatives in the forces. Those who come in good faith confess their sins after three or four inquests, the others get violently kicked out of the camp."[17]

Optimism and excitement surrounded Maceo's preparations to invade the western provinces. The chance to fight alongside the legendary officer was considered a great honor for any soldier. Before the men's departure, their towns organized farewell parties, like the one on October 31, 1895, in Mala Noche for the Holguín families, which had come to say good-bye to their relatives heading out to Las Villas. The women were there to inspire bravery among the soldiers. This was, some thought, the most beautiful period of the Revolution. Never before had the rebel soldiers been so confident of their victory, the Mambisas so supportive of the patriotic cause: "Everything is great and poetic on this day, for the participation of the woman who, transfigured by patriotic love, appears like an emblem of glory, filling the militant with her passionate soul. Her devotion to the republic brings her to the camp, to see the marching masses of easterners led by Maceo. Not one complains of and pleads

Two Mambisas with a rebel flag. Fondo Cubano, Grupos de Mambises, BNJM.

being orphaned, widowed, or other causes to exempt a man from the fight; they all show how proud they are that their men are lucky enough to go with Maceo on the western conquest.[18]

Many of the soldiers carried with them *detentes,* or good luck amulets, to stop bullets, like the one given to Grover Flint, the New York reporter, when he joined the rebels on one of their marches: "It was a little, scalloped strip of white flannel, embroidered in silk with a crimson heart, a green cross, and scroll of leaves, and the motto 'Detente! El corazón de Jesús está conmigo.' [Stop! Jesus' heart is with me.] It was a simple insurgent emblem, such as the busy little fingers of the faithful Cuban maidens in Cardenas stitch in numbers to be sent out secretly to brothers, sweethearts and cousins in the *manigua*."[19]

Maceo's invasion of the western provinces in 1896 succeeded. Amazingly, he and his men were able to break through the highly fortified and patrolled line the colonial government had built to separate the wealthy western provinces from rebel territory. His popularity among the Mambisas was unparalleled. Women of all social classes, both black and white, worshiped the general who had become the very symbol of a free Cuba. They waited for him along the roads where he was expected to pass and cheered his progress into enemy territory. Luciano Franco, Maceo's biographer, recounts that, after Maceo stayed with a prefect's family, the prefect's wife, Lucía, "following the custom of the Cuban women patriots, who adored the hero, kissed Maceo."[20]

Maceo undoubtedly enjoyed his popularity with rebel women. But he also seemed to miss his wife and complained in his letters that she was too busy with women's politics to write to him: "It seems that you've forgotten me. It seems that revolutionary-womanly politics is driving you crazy. God grant that you are healthy and fat."[21]

Tragically for the Cuban rebels, Maceo was killed by the Spanish army in December, 1896. Spaniards in Cuba reacted to Maceo's death with euphoria. Now that the most daring, determined fighter against their rule was gone, they reasoned, the insurrection was doomed. The Cuban people went into mourning. Women, in particular, did not try to hide their grief. They dressed in black and proudly endured insults from the Spanish soldiers.

Maceo's death sent the Cuban exile community into shock. From Paris, Marta Abreu, a wealthy Cuban who, unlike most of the members of her class, supported the rebellion, cabled Tomás Estrada de Palma, who had replaced Martí as head of the New York junta: "Tell me if the devastating news is true. You can count on ten thousand pesos. Onward." She signed her message with the name Ignacio Agramonte, the slain hero of the Ten Years War.[22]

Of all the patriots in exile, none contributed more money to the cause of independence than Marta Abreu. She sent her first contribution in January, 1869. She then cabled thousands of pesos to the New York junta, financed the publication of *La República Cubana*, and underwrote the purchase of guns and even a ship for the rebels. She paid for the passages back to America of Cubans who had been deported to Spain and assisted rebels in and out of jail. She came to the rescue of the revolutionary government again and again when its funds were depleted. "The magnitude of your gift halted my hand and silenced my voice," wrote Tomás Estrada de Palma, after one of Abreu's donations in January, 1897.[23]

Abreu's proindependence views were an extension of her political concerns and interest in social reform. She was born in 1845 in Santa Clara to an extremely affluent family. Once she inherited her parents' fortune, she used it to improve her neighbors' living conditions. Hers was not random charity, but methodically planned philanthropy in line with her political vision of social justice. Like Jane Addams and other American reformers, Abreu believed in

Marta Abreu. Fondo Cubano, Abreu, BNJM.

transforming the environment to allow the growth of an individual's moral character. She financed public works that would benefit large segments of the population. In Santa Clara, it was her money that built a school for white children and another for black children, a children's hospital, a public laundry, a residence for families temporarily out of resources, the fire station, the police station, a theater, a nursing home for the elderly, and a meteorological observatory. She brought lampposts into the town, paid to fix crumbling bridges, and improved roads and public transportation. She supplied the town's library with books and made sure that it stayed open late so that workers could use it at night. Through it all, she remained a private person, always refusing to have her name attached to any of her philanthropic endeavors and seldom attending the grand-opening ceremonies her town staged to celebrate its improvements. According to Mirta Aguirre, Abreu carried out the most complete social philanthropy of any nineteenth-century Latin American woman.[24]

One beneficiary of Abreu's generosity was Manuela Cancino, one of the girls who spent the Ten Years War hiding deep in the mountains and who had been honored in verse by the poet Fornaris. Before the War of Independence broke out, she had worked as a teacher and composed poetry. She joined the anticolonial forces when the conflict erupted and was caught soon after and sent to the Havana jail, Las Recogidas. She was then deported to La Isla de Pinos, leaving a young daughter in care of a sister. Cancino's suffering was ameliorated only by the financial support of Marta Abreu. From Nueva Girona in La Isla de Pinos, Cancino wrote on May 26, 1896: "A year of exile, suffering every sort of vicissitude, is sufficient, I believe, to enervate the bravest of spirits. I had already lost hope of leaving here, and to die, abandoned, of nostalgia and deprivations, was the future that awaited me. I thank you, for what it's worth, for the interest you have taken in sweetening my bitterness. The mere idea that I might possibly return to see my daughter keeps me from staggering before the thousand obstacles which present themselves in this undertaking—but a mother has to brave everything."[25] A year and a half later, and thanks to Marta Abreu's pressure and money, Cancino was finally released from prison. She wrote to thank her benefactor:

My first impulse, after having suffered getting pushed and shoved around every imaginable way—as much in Cuba as on La Isla de Pinos —was to rush to my poor daughter and banish myself voluntarily to Tampa or Key West; but some good friends advise me to stay here two or three months and await new political developments, and not go make myself suffer miseries in a country where I don't even know the ways of the people.... I was in exile for eighteen months and I was able to survive without ever humiliating myself in the face of my oppressors, thanks to your generous gifts. Time will prove that they have not been planted in sterile ground.[26]

Like Manuela Cancino, thousands of Cuban women who collaborated with the insurgent army became political prisoners during the war. Many of them were forced to serve sentences in Las Recogidas, the largest and most infamous women's jail on the island.

The Catholic Church founded Las Recogidas in 1764 as an institution to shelter and help reform prostitutes. By the mid-1800s, its pious objectives abandoned, the place indiscriminately housed common criminals, prostitutes, and political prisoners. Concha Agramonte, already in her sixties, was imprisoned there for her role as Camagüey's agent for the rebel government. So, too, were Rosario Morales and her two daughters, María and Raquel, when the government discovered that their house was the storeroom for thousands of bullets hidden in condensed milk cans, which were delivered throughout the country by train.[27]

One of the most dangerous war activities women performed and one that often landed them in Las Recogidas or in a smaller local prison was that of courier. A woman traveling tended to give rise to fewer suspicions than did a man and could therefore carry messages to the rebel army with a better chance of not being searched. An additional advantage was that the many layers of women's clothing allowed letters, medicines, maps, and other useful material to be carried inconspicuously. Clemencia Arango was one of these couriers.

When Clemencia Arango's older brother joined the rebellion, he wrote to his sister urging her to accept his decision: "I only ask you not to get upset, to continue with your lessons, and to take care of your little brothers and sisters as you have until now, while your brother fights for our country, and until he comes back to embrace you in happier days."[28] Clemencia Arango, however, did more than wait at home for her brother to come back. She became an active emissary and agent for the Cuban Revolutionary Party, time and again slipping through the enemy lines to bring clothes, medicines, weapons, and messages to the soldiers. In early 1897, the colonial government, well aware of Clemencia Arango's political involvement, expelled her from Cuba. The PRC, acknowledging her contributions, came readily to her aid. Tomás Estrada de Palma, head of the New York junta, wrote: "Yesterday I received the letter you sent me from Havana, dated in January, communicating to me the news, which I already had heard from the newspapers, that the Spanish government had ordered you to leave the island of Cuba. People like you are deserving of the party's protection, and I had already anticipated your request. Believing that you would stop in Key West, on Saturday I communicated my instructions to Poyo's [the PRC leader] agent to lend you his services."[29]

Sitting next to her at dinner on the American vessel that carried her into exile was Richard Harding Davis, the flamboyant correspondent for William Randolph Hearst's New York *Journal*. From Arango, Davis learned how the Spanish authorities searched her thoroughly because of their suspicion that she was carrying information for the New York junta. This gave Davis the opportunity to send one of his most forceful dispatches demanding that the United States intervene in Cuba. The *Journal* jumped at this chance with sensationalist headlines: "Does Our Flag Shield Women? Indignities Practiced by Spanish Officials on Board American Vessels. Richard Harding Davis Describes Some Startling Phases of the Cuban Situation. Refined Young Women Stripped and Searched by Brutal Spaniards While under Our Flag on the *Olivette.*"[30] This news was augmented with a Frederick Remington sketch showing a prim young woman forced to undress in front of a group of impudent Spanish officers. Davis encouraged his readers' outrage by dismissing reports in some American papers that rebel women were wild fighters. "I found that she was not an Amazon, or a Joan of Arc, or a woman of the people with a machete in one hand and a Cuban flag in the other. She was a well-bred, well-educated young person who spoke three languages and dressed as you see girls dress on Fifth Avenue after church on Sunday."[31]

As the *Journal* had hoped, a wave of indignation followed the report, and Congress began to discuss a resolution that would prevent Spain from searching women on American steamers. Unfortunately for the *Journal,* Joseph Pulitzer's New York *World,* fuming over its rival's scoop, decided to investigate the accuracy of Davis's accusation. To the *World* reporters' delight, when they interviewed Arango, she told them she had not been strip-searched by male officers, but examined by a police matron in a private room. Davis blamed Remington for embellishing his dispatches. Congress did not introduce the resolution.[32]

We do not know how Clemencia Arango felt about her brief notoriety. Settling in New York, she continued her involvement with the PRC in a variety of ways. As a worker for the Cuban Army Scientific and Relief Medical Club, she was "authorized to solicit drugs, surgical instruments, and all kinds of medical supplies for the use and relief of the Cuban army of liberation."[33] Using "Virginia Lamar" as her nom de guerre, she corresponded with the island's rebels about highly classified material such as the shipment of ammunition.

Various agents, signing their letters as "El Capitán" (The Captain) "Black," or "El Monje" (The Monk), regularly dictated instructions to her on how to send gunpowder, ammunition, medicines, and other items for the insurrection. Bullets purchased in New York and Key West, for instance, were to be sent in the bottom of condensed milk cans. A letter addressed to Virginia Lamar on March 27, 1897, informed Arango of the landing on the Cuban coast of a rebel expedition and how the crew of an armed sloop had joined the insurrection.[34]

Particularly interesting is the intense correspondence she maintained with H. Donnell Rockwell, who worked at the U.S. general consulate in Havana. Regularly throughout the summer and fall of 1897, he kept her informed of the

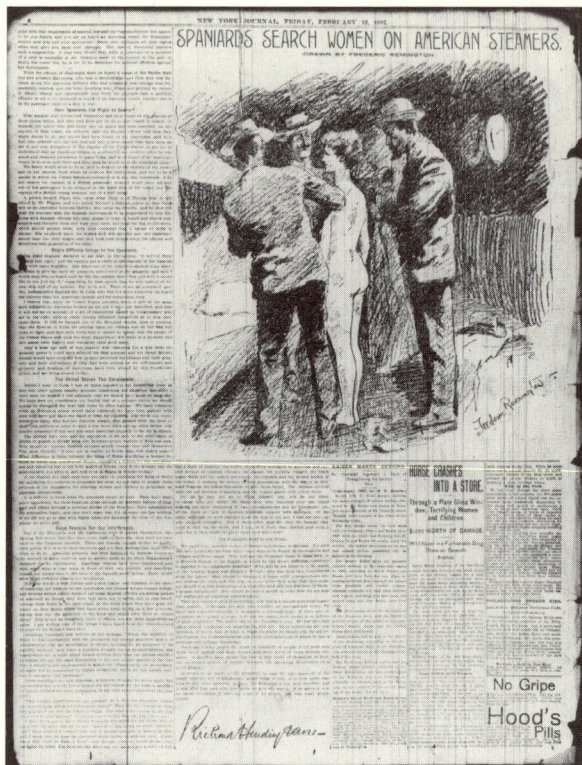

Frederick Remington illustration for the New York *Journal* that supposedly
portrays Clemencia Arango being strip-searched by Spanish men on an
American ship. Library of Congress

political situation of the island—news of Cubans who had been detained for
antigovernment activities, the effect of Spanish policies on the population,
and so on. He also enclosed in his correspondence letters of introduction to
friends in New York to help her with her work. When he was transferred to
the War Department, Rockwell continued his correspondence with Arango
from Washington.[35]

Another prominent revolutionary courier was Magdalena Peñarredonda,
from Pinar del Río, who, as a girl, cut her braids after the execution of Joaquín
de Agüero in 1851. She married a Spanish officer at age fifteen, but later
separated from him. She grew up in El Pontón, her parents' country estate in
Artemisa, a fertile region of rich coffee plantations west of Havana. Her father
was Spanish and had connections to the military. Her mother, who belonged
to a French family that had settled in Cuba after Haiti's revolution, instilled in
her children the liberal views of the French Enlightenment.

During the Ten Years War, Peñarredonda opposed the colonial government, but that conflict never reached the western part of the island, and her participation was therefore limited. By the early 1890s, however, she was a prominent member of the opposition and, at her home, intellectuals, politicians, and war veterans discussed, plotted, and conspired. In fact, the rebel forces turned her house into an arsenal, with her bed, dresser drawers, and flowerpots hiding weapons.

Peñarredonda's proindependence activities, such as the publication of an article in *El Criollo* defending a nationalist position, forced her to move to New York before the war. In the United States, she met José Martí and other leaders of the Cuban exile community. When the War of Independence began in 1895, the New York junta appointed Magdalena as the Pinar del Río delegate, one of the highest political positions held by a woman during the conflict.

Magdalena Peñarredonda served as a courier for many rebel leaders, especially Antonio Maceo, for whom she felt great admiration. She acted as intermediary between the general, his officers, and the rebel government's representatives in Havana. Her responsibilities included handling great amounts of money moving in and out of the island for various war purposes. In 1896, Maceo sent a letter to a high rebel government officer asking him to turn the money in his vaults over to Peñarredonda: "Go deliver to the *delegada* [delegate] the republic's funds that you have in your power, dividing them into parts of two, three, and four thousand pesos, so that she, in turn, can deliver them to Mr. González for the NY delegate (Estrada Palma). If it happens that you can't find said woman, Colonel Sartorio or the messenger will give you accurate information about her residence."[36]

The lively correspondence Peñarredonda maintained with rebel officers gives an indication of the tenor of her preoccupations and contributions. Her letters to Maceo, for instance, include discussions of political strategy. One of their exchanges addresses the role of the U.S. media in helping shape the outcome of the conflict. From Maceo's response we can infer that Peñarredonda realized how crucial the American media could be in helping the rebel cause. Maceo, on the other hand, was unwilling to trust anything but the Cubans' own strength: "It is true that we should grab the foreign press's attention and use it as revolutionary propaganda, if possible. The two important newspapers you mention [most likely Hearst's New York *Journal* and Pulitzer's New York *World*] are undoubtedly the ones that can best serve this purpose, and good proof of this is how hostile they are to the Spaniards and how they insult them daily. Despite this, I'll repeat to you that the key to our definitive success will be our own effort."[37]

Peñarredonda, or "General Llellena," as she was popularly known, crossed the *trocha* almost daily for two years, hiding the rebels' letters, medicines, and other useful items inside her petticoat and a briefcase with a false bottom. Her noms de guerre were "Benito Gómez," "Máximo Juárez," and "Maine," pseudonyms she used on a regular basis as a revolutionary agent. Her correspondence with rebel officers shows that the troops depended on her for food, clothes, medicines, and news. She provided the soldiers items such as shoes, hats, underwear, paper, ink, pens, books, and condensed milk, as well as crucial information for the officers, such as maps and strategic military plans.

In the active correspondence she maintained with the Cuban government in exile, she made it clear that the difficulty of getting medicine was the Achilles' heel of the rebel army. "I have talked to some soldiers who turned themselves in," she wrote to Tomás Estrada de Palma in May, 1897, "and they complained about the lack of medicines, especially quinine. Many blamed their surrender on this lack of medication and on the miserable state they were in because of their fever."[38] The problem, however, was easy to solve, she explained: "I count with fast and safe means to deliver as many packages as you want twice a week to the town of Pinar del Río."[39] Good to her word, Peñarredonda was soon distributing remedies for malaria, dysentery, wound infections, and other health problems that regularly affected Cuban soldiers. Before the end of 1897, she wrote to ask for a new cargo of medicines: "I have managed to open one path from Pinar del Río and one from Consolación to allow communication between those towns and General Díaz."[40] A receipt dated March 19, 1898, shows the success of Peñarredonda's work. On it Gen. Pedro Díaz thanks Peñarredonda for bringing to his camp, among other items, quinine pills, four pounds of soda sulfate, potassium permanganate, a packet of cotton, iodine, and tincture to prevent infections.[41]

An interesting letter from Díaz to Magdalena Peñarredonda shows that, despite her important and dangerous responsibilities as *delegada* and rebel agent, she wisely foresaw the lack of recognition she would receive after the war. We do not know exactly what she requested as reward for her services. Perhaps it was an explicit acknowledgment by rebel officials of her work—which the general trivialized with a reference to her "selflessness and patriotism"—or perhaps a promise of a secure position in the postwar years. Díaz wrote: "With respect to the comments that you have made of your aspirations for the very important work that you have done on behalf of our cause, we know well enough the selflessness and patriotism you have demonstrated on all occasions. As for the affection you expect from us, for my part I have to

Magdalena Peñarredonda (*second from right*). To her right is Gen. Pedro Díaz. Fondo Cubano, Cubanos Distinguidos, Album 101, BNJM

tell you that you have always held a very important place in my heart, and I believe I speak as well for the people surrounding me, though this is a mere trifle in accordance with what you deserve."[42] There is no evidence of whether Peñarredonda found this response sufficiently comforting. But she continued attending to the rebels' needs and denouncing the impact of colonial policies on the rural communities until she was caught and sent to Las Recogidas.[43]

Once again, the war brought devastation to the Cuban countryside. In 1895, to punish the plantation owners who had turned to the Spanish government for support, the rebel army began burning all cultivated fields. While this strategy targeted the big property owners, small landholders were also affected, as the rebels deemed the policy to be more effective if they made no exceptions. That the Cuban peasantry supported the insurgent army despite this policy indicates how strong the anticolonial feeling had become among the rural population by the 1890s, particularly considering that not only the land but also the *guajiros*' houses often were set on fire to ensure that the enemy would not use them as shelters. At times, the peasants themselves would burn their own fields as a way to show their commitment to independence. Or they would ask the rebel soldiers to do it for them. One soldier recounted that at the beginning of the war

General Masó received a visit from a fairly aged woman who had come to place at his disposition the resources of a variety shop that she possessed on the Vicaña road and to ask him to burn the house it was in, which was also part of her property, once the merchandise had been taken out of it. The lady had learned that the enemy was going to send a detachment to set up a post there, and she, a patriot, preferred that her property be destroyed rather than have Spanish forces occupy it. Immediately, the general himself went with a few troops down the road to that place. They put all the useful goods in carts and set the house on fire. The general had wanted to give everything that had been salvaged back to the good woman, but the poor lady did not have anywhere to take it, so it was distributed among the troops.[44]

Not all civilians' responses, however, were so heroic. For many, whether or not they sided with the insurgent army, the burning of everything they owned felt like too high a price to pay, a sacrifice they were not willing to make. Inevitably, tensions arose between these lukewarm supporters and the military. In his war diary entry for October 18, 1895, rebel officer Bernabé Boza, who fought with Gen. Máximo Gómez, included the following anecdote:

The general ordered the family of a man named Carbonell to leave their house and that the house be burned; he couldn't comprehend how a Cuban family could live under the shelter of a Spanish fort. Very strong words flew between Mrs. Carbonell and the general. We marched out at 8 A.M. and encamped in "las lajitas," where I was able to send my wounded men to a hospital. Since it was the general-in-chief's saint's day, everyone who was in the camp congratulated him. He wrote a letter to Mrs. Carbonell explaining to her his conduct and offering her, if she wanted it, pecuniary compensation for the material losses she suffered from the destruction of her house. The woman answered the letter in a severe, laconic, and pitiful manner, making strong accusations against the general's attitude, saying it was too rough. The general refuted these charges, employing indictments of a different kind, in energetic and equally correct language.[45]

We do not have information about Mrs. Carbonell's political views, whether her reaction reflected an antipathy to the rebel cause or whether she was merely angry about the destruction of her property. In any case, the exchange between her and Gómez shows a woman who was incensed enough, but also confident enough, to challenge the top military leader of the rebel army. The fact that he felt compelled to take time on his saint's day to write her a letter offering compensation for her losses reveals a degree of concern or compassion for this woman's plight. But in this case, there was no compromise. She did not accept his apology nor he her accusations.

These two responses to the burning policy reflect the complex interaction between the insurgency and the civilian population. By and large, however, support from the countryside ensured the rebels' survival. While the Spanish army was able to control Cuba's towns and urban centers, it was much harder to control the rural areas. In the countryside, the peasants were in daily contact with the rebel forces, helping the insurrectionists in any way they could. The *guajiras*, or peasant women, opened their homes to the rebels, cooked for them, and washed their clothes. They supplied the soldiers with meat and vegetables, coffee, honey, and candles. In the territory controlled by the rebels, women could occupy the position of "prefects," who were in charge of collecting and distributing food, clothes, weapons, and ammunition. The prefects also directed production at the *talleres* hidden in the mountains, where gunpowder, clothing, saddles, and other war necessities were produced.[46] American correspondent Grover Flint, who spent a few days in one of those enclaves, described how even girls were employed in helping the rebels. One prefect's daughters, "Mercedes and Rosalía[,] made hats for the Cuban soldiers. One twisted strands of bleached grass into a narrow tape and trimmed the edges with small scissors; the other coiled the long neatly woven braid round and

Hat weavers. Fondo Cubano, Album 73, BNJM

round from a central point in the crown, sewing the overlapped edges together till the brim, wide as you chose was finished. Each hat was a good two days' work."[47]

As in the Ten Years War, rural support proved crucial to the Cuban army. The rebels avoided confrontations with the better-equipped Spaniards and favored, instead, a war of surprise skirmishes, a strategy well suited to a small army that was fighting on its native land. Despite its military superiority, Madrid could not defeat an enemy that was nowhere to be found.

In the type of warfare that emerged in the 1890s, those forces that had accurate information about where to find food and shelter, the shortest route to a desired destination, the size of the enemy forces, and, most basically, where the enemy happened to be were at a tremendous advantage. In this role of disseminating information to the rebel forces, the peasant population became a key player. Thanks to the *guajiros'* warnings, the rebels could avoid meeting the enemy unless they were ready for a confrontation. For Spain, the war in Cuba became, as Antonio Elorza and Elena Hernández Sandoica aptly put it, a game of *gallina ciega,* or blindman's buff.[48] The colonial army chased a ghost enemy that materialized only in surprise attacks.

Peasant women took on much of the responsibility for feeding information to the insurgents. As increasing numbers of men joined the rebel forces, the role of women in rural areas became more significant, a fact that did not escape Arsenio Martínez Campos. Martínez Campos, the Spanish general who negotiated the Pact of Zanjón, which ended the Ten Years War, had been sent back to Cuba when the new conflict began. He soon realized that the Cuban peasants' support of the rebel army stood in the way of a Spanish victory. Not even the offer of substantial rewards would incite the peasants to serve his soldiers as guides, he complained. And Spain was not worried merely about the men: "If the risk of men doing espionage is eliminated," he declared, "women and children will do it."[49]

The lack of victories, underscored by the unexpected arrival of Antonio Maceo's men in the western part of the island in January, 1896, was the downfall of Martínez Campos. He was replaced by Valeriano Weyler, who believed that only brutal repression would bring the rebellion to its knees. Weyler responded to the difficulties the Spanish army encountered in the countryside with a policy of *reconcentración,* which forced the rural population to abandon their homes and move to the fortified towns controlled by the government. If the survival of the insurgent forces depended on the support of the Cuban peasantry, Weyler reasoned, then the Cuban peasantry would be removed,

A young Mambisa. Fondo Cubano, Album 74, BNJM

their crops destroyed. In October, 1896, Weyler issued the decree mandating that civilians who lived in the country move into the towns or villages occupied by Spanish troops.

The tragic consequences of this order were soon felt. The Cuban peasants were left with two options: join the rebels, or move into a crowded town where they had almost no means of support. Many peasants—men and women—opted to follow the rebel army as part of the *impedimenta*, a noncombatant army charged with taking care of and transporting cattle and war matériel for the troops. Maceo's army in Pinar del Río, for instance, included about one thousand peasants, two hundred of whom were women.[50]

Most peasant women and their children, however, filed into the government-controlled centers, where they soon faced starvation and disease. The towns were not prepared to receive such a tremendous influx of people, particularly because the *reconcentración* policy put an end to the normal arrival of

An integrated group of rebel soldiers, including two young women in uniform. Fondo Cubano, Grupos de Mambises, BNJM

food from rural areas. Havana became the destination of more than seventy thousand *reconcentrados*, who were forced to live in makeshift camps and to beg for food. Cholera, typhoid fever, dysentery, and yellow fever were their regular visitors.[51] An example of the devastating effect of the *reconcentración* policies is to be found in the information that "the Monk," Clemencia Arango's secret correspondent, sent to her while she was in New York. According to his estimates, in the town of Santa Clara, 78 people died in January, 1897. In February, when the *reconcentración* began, the mortality rate was 114; in March, 333; April, 524; May, 539; and by December, 1897, the number had climbed to 1,011.[52]

American plantation owner Edwin Atkins recalled how doing laundry for the townspeople allowed some women to feed their families. Such jobs, however, were limited. Most found no work whatsoever and had to depend on charity to keep their children alive. Atkins described how he helped feed these destitute women:

Yesterday my "widows," as they are called here, were down for their weekly rations. They all come together as far as the sentry at the gate of the *batey* [living quarters and storerooms in a Cuban sugar mill], where

A group of Mambises. Fondo Cubano, Grupos de Mambises, BNJM

A group of Mambises. Fondo Cubano, Grupos de Mambises, BNJM

they are admitted four at a time. Many had their children with them. Our doctor very kindly offered to treat my widows and orphans free, for which they seemed very grateful, and all took advantage of the offer on the spot, I furnishing medicines. The old judge, the new boss of our freight handlers, to [whom] we have entrusted the distribution of supplies, knows most of the people at Guaos and says many of the people whom I have taken in charge were formerly quite well-off. They were all neatly dressed and seem respectable, as well as respectful, people.[53]

The women's good behavior was rewarded in this case with rice, jerked beef, beans, and salt.

Ramiro Guerra's family was among those forced to abandon its land. The town where they lived during the *reconcentración* had a tobacco factory, which employed a number of peasant women at pitiful wages. His mother was fortunate to find work as a cook for an officer's family.[54] Guerra also left a moving portrait of the desperate plight faced by a young *reconcentrada* from Pinar del Río:

Almost shoeless, covered in tattered rags, she advanced on the old planks covered with splinters and boarded the boat docked on the jetty. She came up to the galley and held out a tin plate in silent supplication. She asked for a few scraps left over from lunch. The cook, brutally lascivious, looked at her and smiled. She approached him, extended her hands. The adolescent's face took on an expression of infinite anguish. She raised her head, perhaps implied a gesture of repulsion or of defense, but her wounded pride showed itself in such a resigned and hopeless suffering that the sacrilegious hand tarried. The plate was filled; a piece of paper covered it. A trembling "thank you" was heard, like a whispered breath, and the *reconcentrada* left, crossing the eaten-away pier, toward the miserable hovels where the moribund fathers and the hungry little brothers awaited.[55]

Magdalena Peñarredonda, in a letter to Tomás de Estrada, conveys her indignation about the effects of the *reconcentración*:

I have returned to Vuelta Abajo twice since General Maceo's death. Believe me, I have witnessed scenes that could not possibly be more horrible and moving in human suffering. Those poor *guajiras* are true heroines, but little by little all that suffering is killing their moral character. The corruption bred by this state of things will drive one insane. Think

of so many poor, hungry women and of that brutal and licentious sol-
diery, all of them crowded into the towns like cattle. Here, even if this
sounds like blasphemy, we are forced to doubt God's existence and to
believe in the devil, since only a being as infernal as Weyler can commit
so many horrors.[56]

The towns tried to address the needs of the newcomers by distributing one
meal per day—usually consisting of bones and beans. It was almost impossible
to find milk for the children. Women's clubs tried to alleviate the plight of the
reconcentrados by raising money for them. Edelmira Guerra, founder of the
revolutionary Esperanza del Valle Club in Cienfuegos, issued communiqués
that denounced the colonial government's policy as an extermination of the
Cuban people. She encouraged women to sell their jewelry and to donate the
profits to help feed the hungry and to support the cause of independence. In a
daring move, Guerra and her club members visited Weyler to ask for money
for the needy, without revealing, of course, their involvement in the anticolonial struggle.[57]

While death and starvation marked the lives of those living in the towns,
the countryside had turned into a wasteland. Weyler matched Gómez's torch
policy by burning every tiny field, every little conuco that could help feed the
rebels. If the peasants had been able to provide the insurgent soldiers with

A group of reconcentrados. Fondo Cubano, Reconcentrados, BNJM

vegetables and meat in the early stages of the conflict, *reconcentración* made finding food and shelter almost impossible. With thousands of hungry soldiers from both sides stomping across the land, and with no *guajiros* to help them, the Mambí rebels were reduced to eating lizards, yams, and mangos.

Also under attack were the workshops where supplies for the army were produced. Even clothing the soldiers became a challenge. This lack of resources affected the women who lived in army camps. José Isabel Herrera wrote: "We had about twenty [women] who were also half naked, having over their bodies only a skirt and a jacket, revealing the entire waist area. These women served the Liberation Army, caring for the wounded and doing so much to help the soldiers not get caught by the enemy, and the general thought they were worthy enough to have someone go look for better clothes for them. Clothes were taken from the people of a farm and distributed to the Mambisas."[58]

An even more urgent problem was finding medicine, particularly quinine, the remedy for the malaria that plagued the soldiers' camps. As in the previous war, in remote areas the Mambí army set up hospitals that were often run by women. One of these nurses was the experienced Rosario Castellanos, the *bayamesa* who had been of great service to the rebels in the Ten Years War. Two decades later, Rosa was back in the *manigua*, this time with the rank of captain of military health (capitán de sanidad militar) and once again managing a makeshift hospital in the Sierra de Nasa. Her expertise in medicinal plants, including a rich variety of mushrooms, ferns, lichens, shrubs, roots, and trees, and her resourcefulness with home remedies made her an invaluable asset to the insurgents. Carlos Muecke Bertel, an American who fought with the rebels, had no complaints about the treatment he received at Castellanos's hospital: "The captain nurses all the sick and wounded men with maternal care and without distinction of rank or color. The meals here are plentiful and tasty. Every now and then the captain hands me a cigar."[59]

In 1898, Castellanos's story made its way into the pages of the New York *Journal*. Reporter Grover Flint, who was covering the war, featured her in one of his dispatches. He had met, he reported proudly, "the celebrated Rosa, known widely through the district for her skill as a nurse and her knowledge of medicinal herbs. In an acre of forest La Rosa could find remedies for every ill. From the shoots of a tiny shrub she made a tea equal to quinine in checking a fever; from a bark of a certain tree she made a plaster that would stop any hemorrhage. She had plants at her command that supplied her with antiseptics and sleeping draughts." In a footnote, the correspondent commiserates

Rosario Castellanos. Reproduced from García, "La mujer en la guerra"

over losing his notes about Rosa's medicinal knowledge: "I made a careful list of Rosa's drugs, with the names of the roots and trees from which she compounded them; unfortunately for the advancement of science, it was lost with some other correspondence."[60]

Isabel Rubio, born in Pinar del Río in 1837, also served in the field as a nurse. Isabel married at age sixteen and reared four children. She spent most of the Ten Years War in Key West, to which her family had been forced to immigrate because of their anticolonial position. She became involved in the political life of the Cuban exile community and met many of its leaders. Returning to Cuba at the end of the Ten Years War, she began to conspire with the rebels. In 1895, she joined the Cuban Revolutionary Party. A charismatic leader, she convinced many important families to join the rebel side, turning Pinar del Río into a revolutionary enclave.

At the age of fifty-eight, Isabel Rubio moved to the *manigua* with her husband, son, and grandson. "I have to practice what I preach," she explained.[61] There she established a mobile hospital staffed with a group of women whom she trained. For bandages, they used torn dresses, blouses, and sheets that rebel women had donated. For medicines, she used plants and herbs whose healing value had been unearthed by her father, a doctor and botanist. For three years, her mobile hospital crisscrossed the Cuban jungle, taking care of the sick and wounded under the most inauspicious circumstances. Traveling through swamps, mountains, and marshes, often in heavy rain, Rubio and her assistants covered hundreds of kilometers and survived on little more than *curujey* (a parasitic plant that grows on the bark of trees) and wild vine lianas. They tended to innumerable malaria cases and used whatever herbs they could find as medicines, such as boiled yam leaves for smallpox and orange tree thorns to pierce the patients' purulent sores. To mend broken bones Rubio relied on fresh palms tied with strips of *majagua* (a tropical tree with strong and flexible wood native to the Antilles).

In 1896, General Maceo, traveling through Paso Real de Guane on his way to the western campaign, stopped to visit Rubio and granted her the rank of captain of military health. Two years later, in February of 1898, the enemy discovered her hospital. "Don't shoot. We are only women, children, and sick men," she shouted. But she was shot in her leg and died three days later of gangrene.[62]

Isabel Rubio's death illustrates the dangers nurses faced. Without uniforms or visible symbols to identify them as medical personnel, without the backing of an international group that would give them neutral status, the nurses were at the mercy of the colonial army and its collaborators. Not surprisingly, as a matter of self-preservation, the line between the women's roles as nurses and as soldiers was often crossed. Taking care of the wounded required defending them, by force, if necessary.

Adela Azcuy is an example of the double role women played as nurses and soldiers. Adela was a passionate chess player and poet and had acquired extensive botanical and medical knowledge working at her husband's pharmacy. An excellent horsewoman, she spent hours, sometimes days, traveling by herself through remote mountainous areas collecting plants that she could use as remedies. She was said to have the most complete collection of native ferns in Cuba. Her sympathy for the cause of independence was well known—she wore her hair down and blue in her clothing, two unmistakable signs of being a Mambisa.[63] When the war began, Azcuy asked to be enrolled as a soldier in the Mambí army, but was denied this privilege and admitted, instead, as a member of the medical team. Soldier or not, by the end of the war, Azcuy could boast of having fought in forty-nine battles. Interestingly, both she and her husband, a Spaniard from whom she separated, rose to the rank of captain in opposing armies.[64]

Adela Azcuy. Reproduced from García, "La mujer en la guerra"

Paulina Ruiz, from Matanzas Province, asked to join the rebel army along with her husband. The officers, after discussing the matter, decided to let her march with the animals in the rear as part of the *impedimenta.* "I did not come here to look at the soldiers' backs," she protested. She was then given the role of standard-bearer, but she often exchanged the flag for a machete. Having nearly lost her life twice in battle, she was rewarded for her bravery in combat with the rank of captain.[65]

Grover Flint describes Ruiz in *Marching with Gomez* (1898). Flint's description confirms the American belief that there were beautiful, fierce Amazons fighting with the rebels. After presenting an embellished version of the many dangers she faced, the machete charges she led, the enemies she killed, the horses shot out from under her, the reporter goes on to explain that Ruiz "wore a linen coat and a short skirt that showed a pair of striped trousers beneath. She was 21 years old and very pretty, with regular features, soft dark eyes, glossy black hair that curled over her forehead, and a gentle, persuasive voice. She was slim as a poplar and very graceful."[66]

Flint created this romantic image of a stylish female warrior for his American audience. There were in fact scores of female fighters with the rebel army.

Rebel group that includes black and white, men and women. Fondo Cubano, Grupos de Mambises, BNJM

Most of them were poor and black. For one thing, poor black women tended to live in rebel camps, whereas it was easier for white women, traditionally with more economic resources, to find safer shelter. María Hidalgo, a black woman from Matanzas, joined the insurgent army in 1895 and for more than two years fought alongside men in many battles. Shot seven times, she was promoted to the rank of captain, a distinction granted to about twenty women.[67]

Most of the names and deeds of the women who fought in battle have gone unrecorded, however. At best, these women are identified by their first name. Manuel Piedra Martel wrote about a young woman named Isabel who was wounded in the battle of Tapia on April 14, 1896:

I was looking at a soldier who was on the ground, a soldier from the escort convoy from the general's division. It was Isabel, a little black girl, who, thanks to her youth, her feminine form not being so well pronounced, and her being dressed like a man, had the look of a boy; thanks also to her seriousness and composure, she had achieved what no other woman had—she had served under General Maceo's command. She was wounded, and her horse had bolted. In these "save yourselves if you can" first moments, she had screamed in vain for someone to come back for her, not to abandon her. I got off my horse, put her on the saddle in front of my seat, and continued with her until we met up with another horseman, whom I ordered to take her and to get her out of danger. After that, Isabel, who had been a fearless combatant, did not reappear on the field of battle. She dedicated herself from then on to working as a nurse in the hospitals.[68]

In his war memoirs, José Isabel "Mangoche" Herrera recalls four women fighting in his regiment. One of them, a seventeen-year-old named Goyita, rushed in battle to save a lieutenant who was surrounded by the enemy when his horse was killed. As she retreated with him on the back of her horse, her hair, which had been pulled up inside her hat, got loose, revealing, to the enemy's surprise, that she was a woman.[69]

But more often than not, the women are simply not identified in any way. A rebel soldier recounted that, on one occasion, when a group of Cuban fighters was trapped in a lagoon of the savanna and the Spanish soldiers had begun to gun them down, a small *mulata*, dressed like a man, rushed to their help, screaming at her comrades: "'Are you men or are you cowards? Are you going to let them kill those poor little Cubans!? If there is anyone here who wants to see how a valiant woman dies, let them follow me!' and she charged quickly without looking to see how many would follow her. She cut down four or five Spanish soldiers with her Paraguayan machete. The Cubans who were buried in the mud were saved by that daring woman." Although the soldier remembered with precision the date of this event—March 2, 1896—the place where it happened, the names of the general, brigadier, and three colonels who commanded the columns, he admitted: "I don't remember the name of the woman."[70]

Women's military participation, especially white women's, challenged nineteenth-century assumptions about female weakness, modesty, and compassion. The war years, when so many social practices were interrupted, so many traditions altered, gave women hope that they now had a chance to redefine gender roles. Like Ana Betancourt and Emilia Casanova during the Ten Years War, Edelmira Guerra, the Mambisa who asked Weyler to donate money for the *reconcentrados*, worked to expand opportunities for women in this new conflict. In 1891, before the war began, from the platform provided by her club, Esperanza del Valle, Edelmira Guerra publicized her vision of the new society that should emerge once Cuba was free from Spanish rule. Her demands included public education for children and adults, separation of church and state, and "the reintegration to women of their natural rights, such as the right to vote for single women over twenty-five and widows, the right to di-

Aurelia Castillo with her Spanish husband, Julián González.
Fondo Cubano, Castillo, BNJM

vorce when there is a good cause, the opportunity for women to work as public
employees, etc., according to physiological and social causes."[71]

In 1895, she wrote to the rebel government asking it to include women's
suffrage in the Constitution. Representatives refused to oblige. In 1901, Esperanza del Valle asked the newly elected Constitutional Assembly to grant Cuban
women the right to vote. Once again, these women were turned down.[72]

Aurelia Castillo also had high hopes for what the revolutionary atmosphere
would do to improve women's status. In 1895, a few months before Valeriano
Weyler's government expelled her from the island for involvement in the independence movement, she wrote of the new woman being born of the ashes of
the dying century: "A great revolution, among various others, is coming about.

Women are demanding their rights. They have been the last slaves of this civilized world. No, something even worse than that: They have been, until now, the laughable sovereigns of a society that is gallant and brutal at the same time."[73]

In an analysis not unlike American feminist Charlotte Perkins Gilman's, Castillo reflected on the suffocating lives most Cuban women led. Man's physical power, she argued, had given him unfair authority over women. Having most sources of income closed to them, women had only marriage as a career. As beauty was the most valuable asset in the marriage market, the competition for husbands had turned women into live mannequins. And once they married, having no power of their own unless granted by their spouses, women found themselves at the mercy of their families. If it was true that many homes were a wife's haven, equally true was that they could also become prisons. She wrote: "Many homes have been paradises for the wife; for mothers, many have been altars. But for each of these, as many have had the ribbon around their flowers traded in for shackles! As many have had their own sons become tyrants!"[74]

The limitations in a woman's life, she argued, had diminished the physical energy on which independence and dignity were based. Those limitations had made women hypersensitive creatures who handed down to their daughters nothing but excessive worries, absurd hygiene, sentimentalism, and a fear of innovation. Burdened by physical and emotional weakness, bound by laws and tradition, Cuban women, she claimed, often resorted to violence as their only way to deal with marital incompatibility: "Infinite numbers of homes have burst into violent protests, scandalous quarrels."[75]

The solution was to create a society with a more equitable distribution of rights and obligations. She had seen thrilling examples of greater gender equality in her travels. In 1893, after visiting the Chicago World's Fair, she reported to her readers in Cuba: "What a pleasure it is to see women here [the United States] driving their own carriages, by themselves or with a friend or young daughter, and to see them move quickly by bicycle without their skirts getting in their way. . . . Even fashion now wants women's dress to have a masculine touch without losing its charm."[76]

Aurelia Castillo's enthusiasm contrasted with Martí's highly critical views of how the gender gap was closing in the United States. José Martí, who lived most of his exile in New York, viewed with dismay what "equality" was doing to North American women. Considering motherhood and professional work to be incompatible, he argued that female teachers, doctors, lawyers, and artists failed to nurture their children properly. The disintegration of domestic happiness and society's moral fiber once women were incorporated into the workplace was, he warned, inevitable. "Women's influence in the republic's masculine trades and businesses is growing with singularity," he wrote, "while the health of the home and the sanctity of existence diminish visibly. It is chilling to look into their [women's] souls."[77]

Martí viewed womanhood as a symbol of purity, motherhood, beauty, and sensitivity. Women were love rather than reason. The care and delicacy Cuban men exhibited when dealing with their wives and daughters, he said, was absent in U.S. society: "The home in this land is not the serene harbor where daughters are a gift and not a burden, and their marriage something to be dreaded, and not wished for. They are, rather, lodging houses, where the management does not believe itself obliged to maintain the guests it has brought into the house. The women in those towns are not born the same way they are in ours, closely watched by the vigilant eyes of their family members, who handle them with gentleness and care."[78]

He was in favor, however, of both women's education and their right to vote. Using an argument also brandished by the American suffrage movement, Martí evoked women's moral superiority: "The Cuban woman has not forgotten how to help her husband tighten his machete in their palm tree houses! And since she knows more about virtue than the man does, she should have the same right to vote. The fatherland belongs to everyone, and it is just and necessary that we never deny any virtues a seat in it."[79]

Ideologists for the Cuban cause, aware of the need to incorporate women into their struggle if the rebellion was to succeed, found themselves on slippery ground when trying to combine traditional Cuban views of womanhood with the new female responsibilities imposed by the war. The danger of "women's liberation" made many committed nationalists nervous. As Nancy Hewitt argues, Cuban men approved of women's activism and "applauded their militancy" because they viewed them as comrades fighting for the same nationalist goals.[80] The view of rebel women as sacrificing mothers, wives, and daughters who overcame their natural weakness and met the revolutionary challenge with bravery was a comfortable image for the supporters of Cuba Libre; anything beyond that image was problematic. They were, after all, revolutionary or not, men and women imbued in nineteenth-century assumptions, one of which was that women had no intrinsic strength and aspirations.

Luz Noriega, young and attractive, was a woman whose fortitude was viewed as an anomaly that made her comrades uncomfortable. Married to a doctor,

Luz Noriega. Reproduced from García, "La mujer en la guerra"

in 1896 she accompanied him to the *manigua* to help care for the sick and wounded. Her work included writing down the names of the fallen soldiers and the type of wound they had died from, a task she performed, to the amazement of the men, without flinching. She lived through skirmishes and battles and was greatly admired for her calm. She was also criticized for it. Her bravery, some men complained, was unnatural in a woman. There was something masculine about her attitude. "I admire her feminine beauty," one reporter wrote, "but I do not like her masculine valor. In a camp, a woman sees and hears what a lady should not see and hear."[81]

Gen. Bernabé Boza also left disapproving comments about Noriega in his war diary. He wrote that the battlefield was no place for a woman—particularly if she was young and pretty.[82] And in his war memoirs, Col. Cosme de la Torriente mentions how once, in the confusion that followed an enemy's attack, the men ran to pick up their horses while Noriega continued to collect the company's provisions, despite flying bullets. "This woman has great courage," he wrote, "but the fact is that I do not like her, and I do not know whether it is simply because of how surprised I am to see her in the force. I believe I have already written that she is young and fairly attractive."[83]

Another soldier, Alfonso Camín, left behind a more sympathetic description. He remembered seeing "Luz's young and beautiful figure on a horse, with her clean dress of *holanda cruda*, her Mambí hat, gun and machete at her cinch." Her striking presence, he reminisced, had made General Maceo exclaim admiringly: "Here comes the Queen of Cuba!" (¡Aquí viene la reina de Cuba!)[84]

Noriega did not want to leave her husband, who suffered from tuberculosis, a condition made worse by the hardships of war. On a quiet day in 1897, he was resting in a clearing while the women were doing laundry, when the enemy found them. The Spanish officer ordered Noriega's husband executed. "My husband is a doctor," she pleaded. "His mission in this war has not been to kill. On the contrary. He has done good by curing people. Why do you condemn him to death?" Her plea disregarded, she then asked that he be killed in her presence, so "that when he dies he has with him a friend's presence: mine." She kissed him good-bye and saw his neck severed with a machete.[85] Noriega was sent to jail and returned to the battlefield when released. In 1901, she committed suicide.

Between 1895 and 1898, the war's devastation touched Cuban women with previously unknown intensity. While the Ten Years War had affected only the eastern regions, the violence of this conflict spread throughout the island. Most victims of the *reconcentración* were women and their small children.[86] Women's political participation was more intense than ever before. In the Ten Years War, by and large, they were drawn to the conflict as a result of their fathers' or husbands' involvement. In the War of Independence, however, women joined the rebellion with a new level of personal commitment. The number of women's clubs and revolutionary activities multiplied. So did the number of women who acted as messengers for the rebel troops, as prefects and delegates. Reflecting women's leading role were the soaring numbers of female prisoners who packed the colonial prisons, particularly Las Recogidas in Havana. One of these women would be "adopted" by the American media and turned into a cause, a cause that would pave the way for the United States to enter the war against Spain and shape Cuba's future.

8

▲▼▲▼▲

Evangelina Cossío Cisneros and the Yellow Press

Of all the Cuban women who played a role in their island's struggle for independence, none achieved the notoriety of Evangelina Cossío Cisneros, a young woman from Havana. The years leading to the American intervention in Cuba were a glamorous age for journalism in the United States. Reporters did not just record what they saw but also interacted with their subjects and affected the outcome of events. Their daring participation in the midst of danger made journalists, particularly war correspondents, famous. Awestruck readers followed their adventures in turbulent, faraway places and trusted their accounts.

Characteristic of the new style of journalism was a predilection for sensationalism. Newspaper editors, in their desire to increase sales, had no qualms about crossing the lines between fact, exaggeration, and pure fabrication. Critics coined the phrase "yellow journalism" to describe this type of reporting, which drove the American media in the 1890s. The fierce competition among local newspapers aggravated the problem. Editors—in an attempt to attract readers' attention on the newsstand—printed juicy, startling, and often inaccurate stories.

Two New York papers, the *World* and the *Journal*, and the two men behind them, Joseph Pulitzer and William Randolph Hearst, embodied this turn-of-the-century media rivalry. And because newspapers throughout the country regularly reprinted stories from Pulitzer's and Hearst's papers, their journalists were able to shape political perceptions at a time when the printed word was nearly the only means of transmitting news. Pulitzer and Hearst both understood how Cuba's turmoil could be translated into increased profits, thus compelling them to mount a feverish campaign for American intervention.

By the mid-1890s, Cuba's struggle for independence from Spain had had a long and dramatic history, but few Americans had paid much attention. The yellow press turned the Cuban problem from an obscure conflict in a Spanish colony into a cause for which Americans would passionately go to war. For American newspapers, the most effective way to capture readers' imagination was through stories that reflected the human dimension of the conflict. Papers focused on the tragic consequences that Spanish rule was having on the Cuban people. Valeriano Weyler's cruel policy of *reconcentración* provided journalists with ample opportunities to shock their U.S. readers. But the most successful approach to awakening American solidarity and promoting a war against Spain proved to be the exploitation of traditional notions of womanhood. Appealing to the need to save women in distress struck a deep chord with the American public.

Hearst's and Pulitzer's men in Havana titillated their readers with descriptions of beautiful and fierce Amazons who fought, machete in hand, at the rebels' side. The story Grover Flint wrote about Paulina Ruiz is one example. Richard Harding Davis's report, and Frederick Remington's accompanying sketch, of how Clemencia Arango had allegedly been stripped and searched by Spanish soldiers aroused the country's sense of moral indignation. The public clamored for more stories on Cuban women as vulnerable victims of Spanish cruelty, and the correspondents delivered, appealing to both the warlike instinct and the chivalry of American manhood. "Down with Woman Slayers" was a popular war cry interventionists used to promote the cause of war. But the most astute use of a Cuban woman to feed the war fever must be credited to William Randolph Hearst and his New York *Journal* for the media extravaganza he created around the story of Evangelina Cossío Cisneros, a young Cuban prisoner.

Evangelina Cisneros, as she became known in the United States, was the daughter of a Cuban rebel who, in 1895, as punishment for his political involvement, had been deported to La Isla de Pinos with his family. Young and attractive, Evangelina caught the eye of Colonel Bérriz, the top Spanish official of the garrison, who soon began to court her. Aware of the colonel's infatuation, a group of exiled rebels conspired with Evangelina to trap the officer.

Evangelina Cossía Cisneros. Reproduced from *The Story of Evangelina Told by Herself.* Photo courtesy of The Newberry Library

They asked the young woman to invite him into her house, where some rebels would be hiding with weapons. Once Bérriz was caught alone and defenseless, he would be forced to surrender the garrison to the insurrectionists. Evangelina agreed to the plan without giving it much thought. "Only my age and my absolute lack of understanding could have induced me to attach myself to such an enterprise," she told a Cuban reporter many years later. "The truth is that I took part in this plot without thinking it through, but with knowledge of what it was."[1]

Things did not turn out as planned. She did her part by enticing Bérriz to her home. "There you have him," she shouted to the fourteen men who were hiding nearby. "You, men, take care of the situation. I can't do anything else."[2] At that moment, however, shots were heard in the distance, creating confusion and indecision among the rebels. Not knowing what was happening, the men left to find out, abandoning their plan and leaving Evangelina in the hands of a livid Colonel Bérriz. She was charged with treason and sent to Las Recogidas prison to await trial.

Evangelina was able to reach Donnell Rockwell, Clemencia Arango's contact at the U.S. consulate, and she asked him to help her escape. Rockwell wrote to Clemencia Arango: "I saw Evangelina yesterday, as I have a special permit. She does not look well. Prison life is telling on her, and there seems to be no immediate prospect of her liberty."[3]

Rockwell told the *Journal* about her predicament. Hearst had been looking for a cause Americans could rally around that would increase his paper's sales. With her beauty, youth, and innocence—painstakingly highlighted by reporters—Evangelina had all the trappings of a romantic heroine. Her sad fate awoke compassion in American women and aroused chivalry in American men. Within a few months she had become the darling of the American media, transformed by the *Journal* into the personification of Cuba itself.

The *Journal*'s campaign to save Evangelina was a sophisticated media circus. The paper portrayed her, in the best Victorian fashion, as a pure, innocent maiden who had been sent to jail for repelling the advances of a lascivious Spanish officer, a fact confirmed in her so-called autobiography, which William Randolph Hearst published and "dedicated to the women of America." She was declared the most beautiful girl in Cuba, as pure as a nun. The editors of Pulitzer's New York *World*, no doubt envious of not having found this gold mine themselves, reported that the American consul in Havana, Fitzhugh Lee, had visited the girl and found her prison conditions acceptable. But readers found the *Journal*'s early account of Evangelina sharing her abode with some of "the most depraved Negresses in Havana" and with "destitute blacks" more appealing.[4]

Lee was quoted in the *World* as saying that the girl would have long been released were it not for all the agitation on her behalf. "That she was implicated in the insurrection of the Isle of Pines there can be no question," he said, adding that she had written to him acknowledging that fact.[5] The *World* also contested the *Journal*'s claim that Evangelina had received a twenty-year sentence by printing a cable from a fuming Weyler, who said that, since Cisneros had not yet been tried, no sentence had been imposed.[6]

Hearst and his men paid no attention to such trifles. The *Journal* launched a campaign to collect signatures to demand Evangelina's release and gathered more than twenty thousand, including those of President McKinley's mother and other prominent women, such as Julia Ward Howe and Mrs. Jefferson

Davis. The crusade to save Evangelina spread to England, transported across the Atlantic by the American Temperance Society. Even Pope Leo XIII petitioned the Spanish authorities for mercy. As expected, newspaper sales soared.

Riding the coattails of the *Journal*'s campaign, in 1897, Virginia Lyndall Dunbar published *A Cuban Amazon*, an allegedly historical novel with the young Cuban woman as its protagonist. Dunbar writes in the preface that hers is an accurate depiction of events: "The statements have all been sworn to, and their truthfulness is not to be doubted."[7] According to Dunbar's account, prior to being jailed, Evangelina Cisneros was a Cuban Amazon. In fact, she had been elected the leader of a whole army by her comrades-in-arms. And although she recoiled from accepting such power, her father's arguments convinced her to take on the responsibility. "Evangeline!" [her father] said, "your countrymen and countrywomen have spoken, and both ask you to lead them. Is it for a Cisneros to retreat when his country calls? No! *Mia Cara!* You have chosen your course and you must not shrink from going wherever it may lead you!"[8]

Casting aside her shyness, Evangelina, or Evangeline, as she is named here, bravely fulfills her responsibility as the insurgents' captain. But she does so on two conditions: "One is that our Amazons share equally all duties with their male brethren; and the other that the latter promise to shield and protect them from insult by either friend or foe!"[9] This Amazon's contradictory demands— expecting both equality with the men and protection by them—captures the duality of Evangelina's American personification. A beautiful young woman warrior was a thrilling—and erotic—image. Yet only by obeying the rules of female propriety could she be a comfortable figure to rally around.

Readers' interest in Evangelina increased when the *Journal*, with the help of Cuban rebels, managed to plot her escape. On October 10, 1897, the *Journal*'s headlines proclaimed the good news: "Evangelina Cossio Cisneros is at last at liberty, and the *Journal* can place to its credit the greatest journalistic coup of this age. It is an illustration of the methods of new journalism, and it will find an endorsement in the heart of every woman who has read of the horrible sufferings of the poor girl who has been confined for 15 long months in Recogidas prison."[10]

The American journalists who helped Evangelina escape did so with the aid of Carlos Carbonell, a Cuban businessman who contributed generously to the rescue operation and offered his home as the young woman's hiding place, though the *Journal* never acknowledged his role.[11] Also involved was Donnell Rockwell, Clemencia Arango's correspondent at the U.S. consulate. He wrote to her with delight: "My Dear Clemencia, By the time this reaches you the splendid news will have come to you of the escape from the Casa de Recogidas of the famous Cuban girl, Evangelina Cossio y Cisneros, about whom the papers have said so much. The affair has naturally made a tremendous stir here. Of course I am very proud that the plan was accomplished so successfully. Rockwell's comments and involvement confirm the behind-the-scenes U.S. support of the Cuban rebellion already suggested by his previous exchanges with Clemencia Arango.[12]

Freeing the Cuban prisoner was, indeed, a perfect example of journalism as understood by Hearst. The reporter became a fearless participant in the events he was covering; his adventures, in turn, became worth reporting. In covering Evangelina's escape from prison with the help of reporter Karl Decker, the *Journal*, all restraint abandoned, provided its readers with an exhaustive description of the event: the secret meetings between Decker and his accomplices; the exchange of letters between Evangelina and her rescuers; the failure of various early plans; the tranquilizer she used to drug her cell mates; the sawing of the prison bars; the boy's clothes she wore as disguise; her boat ride to the United States.

The *Journal* fully understood, in addition to the good read provided by the flight, the story's rich political symbolism. Confronted by a helpless, innocent victim of Weyler's brutality, the paper suggested, the chivalrous United States could not but come to her rescue. While Evangelina became the personification of Cuba, Decker, her rescuer, was portrayed as the embodiment of the United States, a man, American readers were told, with "the Constitution in his backbone, and the Declaration of Independence in his eyes."[13]

The late nineteenth century saw the erosion of some long-held gender assumptions, but the notion that women needed men to protect them was seldom questioned. The media highlighted women's weakness and vulnerability to justify the need for intervention. Cuba, transformed in the American imagination into a female as personified by Evangelina Cisneros, needed to be rescued by American manhood, which Karl Decker so well embodied. Another Victorian feminine quality—modesty—was also presented as moral justification for U.S. intervention. Evangelina's plight was due not so much to her proindependence views as to her virtuous repulsion of the colonel's sexual advances. Seizing this golden opportunity, the Cuban expatriate community confirmed the view of Evangelina as a helpless female. From Key West, *Revista Cayo Hueso* declared: "If the face is the soul's mirror, Miss Cossío Cisneros's face is her best defense. It reveals that she is a little weak girl incapable of plotting revolutionary plans to kill Colonel Bérriz in her home."[14]

W. Joseph Campbell questions whether the rescue helped promote the cause of war and argues that Cisneros was more useful to Hearst as a prisoner.[15] This would be true if Hearst had not exploited the story. It was the liberation of the Cuban girl thanks to the United States, and the possibilities her rescue suggested, that Hearst was after. Having turned the prisoner into a symbol of the island's struggle against the colonial power, the next step was rescuing the island itself. Karl Decker explained in the *Journal*: "Every legal means was tried to gain her freedom, but neither the plea, nor the intercession could call wolf Weyler off his prey. The *Journal* finding that all other methods were unavailing, decided to secure her liberation through force."[16]

Julian Hawthorne writes in his introduction to Evangelina's alleged autobiography: "In the person of Evangelina Cisneros, Cuba appeals to the United States. With what grace can we receive the one and repel the other?" Just like Evangelina, he seems to imply, Cuba should one day be brought under U.S. protection.[17]

Before encouraging any larger action, Hearst needed to defuse any criticism of the *Journal*'s meddling in regard to the Cuban girl. Appealing once again to female compassion, the paper interviewed prominent ladies, all of whom were in agreement about the significance of Evangelina's liberation. Mrs. Ulysses S. Grant stated that Evangelina's rescue would "find an endorsement in the heart of every woman who [had] read of the horrible sufferings of the poor girl."[18] New York governor Bradley's wife declared that true women throughout the civilized world thanked the *Journal* for its noble effort in procuring the escape of the Cuban prisoner. The wife of John Sherman, secretary of state, declared: "The liberation of Miss Cisneros [was] something of which every woman, not only in America, but in the world at large, should be proud." Secretary Sherman, constrained by diplomatic rules from discussing the topic openly, disclosed his support of the rescue with one simple statement: "She is a woman."[19]

Evangelina's rescue was declared to have had no parallel since that of Mary, Queen of Scots. Once safe in American territory, the *Journal* reported, Evangelina again met with her noble rescuer: "They grasped hands and looked into each other's eyes. Then he bent and pressed a kiss upon her forehead. She raised the hand she held to her lips, and for a moment it seemed as though she would sink to her knees. But the rescuer held her erect with his strong right arm. 'None of that,' he was reported to have said gently, 'We are here to rejoice. Let us take the banner of freedom and praise the red, white and blue.'"[20] From the pages of the *Journal*, Julian Hawthorne reminded his readers not to dismiss the fanciful story as a fairy tale: "This is true; it is all real," he wrote.[21]

America showered Evangelina with honors. Her reception at Madison Square Garden, which included an honor guard, musicians, and horse-drawn carriages, was declared "such a demonstration of sympathy for the cause of human liberty as has not been seen in the city of New York since the days of the Civil War."[22] She was even given a reception at the White House, where she reportedly delivered the following speech in front of President McKinley:

> I come to speak to you for the women and children of Cuba, who are helpless. The men, they speak for themselves in the field—but the women and the children—who are the victims of murder and outrage, must look to the great, civilized government of the United States for protection. They ask you that those who are unable to defend themselves against barbarity shall find a defender in the Government of the U.S. The mothers and daughters of Cuba ask you on their knees to save them from further outrage. The women of Cuba will bless you for it.[23]

For the next few weeks, readers were provided all sorts of details about Evangelina's life. The "rescued martyr," as she was often called, was shown in *Journal* sketches wearing an array of clothing, from prison garb to the fancy dresses she wore to the many social occasions the *Journal* organized. To make her suffering more real, the paper also included a sketch contrasting the young woman's healthy looks before her imprisonment (obviously a simple guess, since the illustrator had not seen Evangelina then) and her haggard face after fifteen months in jail.

With great fanfare, Hearst's paper announced that Evangelina had applied for citizenship. According to the *Journal*, she had suggested the idea of becoming an American citizen herself. "Let the *Journal* do me this one more favor," she reportedly said. "I won't ask another, indeed I won't. Please fix it so that I can be made a citizen and please fix it quickly for me, tonight even, if that is possible. I do want to march around and sing 'I am an American.'"[24]

Hearst's men were dispatched to the Naturalization Bureau and had everything arranged for her: flags, flowers, new blotters, pens, and a crowd. She then signed her application and reportedly reaffirmed her determination to become a U.S. citizen. Newspaper readers rejoiced. Such a well-bred, light-skinned, innocent girl was easy to embrace.[25]

Taking advantage of her popularity, the *Journal* pressed on and raised the specter that Spain might demand the prisoner's return. This unlikely possibility was presented as a real danger and unleashed a wave of moral indignation in Americans, who by now saw Evangelina as their charge. As letters from readers demonstrated, the *Journal* had not only aroused general sympathy for Evangelina Cisneros but, in the process, had also provided the American public arguments to justify going to war with Spain.

Throughout the month of October, letters to the editor were printed in which prominent and average readers contemplated and defended an American intervention in Cuba: On October 18, Gov. Joseph F. Johnson of Alabama wrote: "The *Journal* has tried, acquitted and delivered a helpless and innocent woman, surrounded by armed foes in a foreign country. That its action is approved, its fearlessness applauded, and its conduct justified is proven by the fact that the men of the U.S. would go to war rather than see this young woman surrendered to Spain, even if international law should demand that course."[26]

From Pennsylvania, a reader wrote: "I wish to congratulate you on your successful liberation of Miss Cisneros. The thrilling story of her rescue has drawn a new interest to the sufferings of the Cuban patriots and awakened the hope that the U.S. government will do for the 'Gem of the Antilles' what you have done for one of her fair daughters."[27] And from Cleveland: "Keep Miss Cisneros in spite of any demands made by Spain, and shoulder arms if it becomes necessary."[28]

In all, the *Journal* devoted 375 columns to the Evangelina Cisneros affair.[29] As a souvenir, the *Journal* ordered 100,000 coins minted with her profile and the Cuban coat of arms. And why not? With her help, the *Journal*'s profits had tripled and the ground had been laid for U.S. intervention in Cuba.[30] When the American battleship *Maine*, anchored in Havana harbor, mysteriously exploded, killing more than 250 men, Washington blamed Spain and issued a declaration of war. With the enthusiastic support of the American public, the U.S. government dispatched thousands of soldiers to fight the decaying Spanish army in Cuba. The Spanish-American War was a brief confrontation that had far-reaching consequences, altering, as it did, the world's political map. After a humiliating defeat, Spain lost the remains of its empire in Cuba, Puerto Rico, and the Philippines. Spain's retreat from Asia and America signaled the rise of the United States as the leading world power.

The American intervention in 1898 brought Cuba's War of Independence to an end. The United States occupied Cuba for more than three years. When it left, in 1902, the freshly drawn Cuban Constitution included a clause—the Platt Amendment—that assured the American government the right to intervene in the island's internal affairs and thereby underscored the island's weak position vis-à-vis its powerful northern neighbor. This would mark the beginning of a tortuous relationship between the Cuban and the American governments.

Evangelina's name was put to political use one final time in 1925, during the Cuba–United States talks to ratify the Hay-Quesada Treaty. Since 1898, when the War of Independence ended, the American government had maintained an unofficial claim to La Isla de Pinos and encouraged the settlement of American citizens there. When the U.S. delegation discussed its interest in retaining this small island, the Cuban delegate, Cosme de la Torriente, reminded them that this was the site where Evangelina Cossío Cisneros's ordeal had begun and therefore it held special historical significance for the Cuban people. The United States agreed to recognize Cuba's sovereignty over La Isla de Pinos.[31]

Evangelina Cossío Cisneros married Carlos Carbonell, the Cuban businessman who helped finance her escape. When the war was over, she returned to Cuba to live an uneventful life. Fifty years later, in an interview with a Cuban journalist, she still sounded puzzled by all the commotion her case had stirred.[32]

Epilogue

Peace brought relief but also disenchantment to the Mambisas. The political reality for which they fought so hard fell short of their expectations. The rebellion had indeed broken colonial ties, put an end to old-fashioned, outmoded institutions, and ushered Cuba into a modern, secular, capitalist world, but the rebels' ideal of a free Cuba failed to materialize. In the early 1900s, the island tried to define its place as an independent republic in the shadow of an intrusive and powerful neighbor.

When Aurelia Castillo returned to Cuba in 1898, after two years in exile, she found "a grotesque caricature" of the ideals of liberty she had been faithful to all her life.[1] Many Cubans whose high expectations had sustained them through the conflict shared her disappointment. But rebel women had reason to be particularly bitter. Lacking the right to vote or to run for office, once the war was over they lost their political clout. Few received compensation for their role in fighting for their country, and many had to struggle to survive in a society that made little room for women workers. Luz Palomares, for example, who was active in both wars and had achieved the rank of captain in the liberating army, was given a pension, but not until 1931, when she was already in her eighties.[2]

Some women saw their services to the rebellion acknowledged, if only symbolically. When Rosario Castellanos, the nurse who served so competently in both wars, died in 1907, she was buried with military honors in Camagüey.[3] An impressive crowd attended Concha Agramonte's funeral in Puerto Príncipe in 1922.[4] In Havana, Emilia Córdova was honored with a statue for her role as a nurse. And Santa Clara also built a statue to honor the memory of Marta Abreu, the town's wealthy benefactor.

The women who fared best were those who could count on male relatives to take care of them. Those who could not, no matter how important their contribution to the war had been, were left in a vulnerable position. As Lois M. Smith and Alfred Padula point out, war widows had to scramble to find employment as domestic servants, seamstresses, or cigarette makers.[5] It is startling to see how many rebel women ended their lives alone and impoverished. Occasional, brief obituaries in newspapers or magazines record their deaths and show over and over that these women asked for little after the war and received even less. After visiting Ignacio Agramonte's widow, Amalia Simoní, at the end of the War of Independence, Raúl Roa wrote: "She was an heir to fertile and vast land. Now she does not even own the modest roof that lodges her. The implacable wind of war destroyed her copious fortune."[6]

Manuela Cancino, the poet and teacher who had relied on Marta Abreu's generosity while jailed on La Isla de Pinos, left evidence of the hardships she faced in a poem published in *El Fígaro* two years after the war ended:

We don't have a home, my daughter,
we don't have a home
we go through this barren world
without refuge or bread
without a loving, warm hand
to support your orphaned childhood,
we live merely on the thistles
left in your poor gauze.[7]

Manuela died soon after publishing this poem.

Carolina Rodríguez, the Key West tobacco worker who contributed so much to the cause of independence, died in utter poverty. Edelmira Guerra, the founder of the Esperanza del Valle Club, died poor and alone and was buried in a common grave. Candelaria "Cambula" Acosta, who fought with Céspedes in 1868, and Trinidad Lagomasinos, a reputed rebel courier in the 1890s, are among the women who, according to the period's sources, died poor and forgotten.[8]

Soon after the war, Rita Suárez, founder of La Cubanita Club, which had played such a critical role in the Cienfuegos area, wrote to Máximo Gómez seeking a position as a schoolteacher in Havana. She had a teaching certificate, she explained, and the people's support, but not the mayor's sympathies, because she had protested a brothel in her neighborhood. "I don't ask for it as a reward for my patriotic work," she wrote, "but because of my desire to help my family."[9] Three months and three letters later, she was still pleading: "With my heart full of disenchantment, I am bothering you again to see if you can do something for me here in Havana or in Cienfuegos."[10] She finally got her wish when she was appointed principal of a school for girls.

Most Mambisas kept any feelings of betrayal to themselves. Not so Magdalena Peñarredonda, who loudly voiced her anger in articles and essays she published throughout the early 1900s. A few months before the war ended, Peñarredonda was caught and imprisoned in Las Recogidas. While in jail, she became the spokesperson for the prisoners by denouncing the women's dismal living conditions and advocating for more humane treatment.[11] From her cell, she followed the American intervention and the end of the war with skepticism: "Americans finally intervened," she wrote to a rebel general, "and what good business it's been for them. Their acts, according to President McKinley, are inspired by *pure love* of humankind. We'll see if future events prove this to be true."[12]

After gaining her freedom, Peñarredonda tried to continue supporting the revolutionary effort: "You know that I am willing to help you in everything," she wrote to another general, "anything you need, let me know with all frankness, as you would talk to a comrade."[13] But she soon realized the new society had no interest in her help. Revolutionary ideals such as heroism, self-sacrifice, and responsibility to the homeland that had glued the rebels together throughout the wars began to sound old-fashioned and incongruous in postwar Cuba. Peñarredonda's frustration at the outcome of events was exacerbated by the fact that her active involvement in the war was never rewarded. On May 26, 1903, she complained in a letter to a local paper: "I don't even have a place to work, where I can devour the bitterness that the absorbing and sterilized selfishness of some revolutionaries and many 'yes-sir-patriots' cause me."[14]

Magdalena Peñarredonda confided her anger to her friend María Cabrales, widow of Antonio Maceo. While much of that correspondence has been lost, we get a glimpse of Cabrales's feelings about postwar Cuban politics from a letter she wrote to Peñarredonda. After wishing her a Merry Christmas and best wishes for the upcoming year of 1903, María Cabrales confesses: "As for me, I can tell you that I am exhausted, my spirit overwhelmed by so much human misery. The only consolation that I have is that we have to die inevitably, and all arrogance and vanity fades before this fact of life."[15]

It can be argued that only a small minority of Cubans—men or women—who fought in the wars received recognition for their involvement. Black soldiers, for example, who achieved a significant level of respect during the military conflict, once the War of Independence was over found themselves constrained by racial prejudice. Commiserating about the difficulties that black Cubans encountered in the increasingly racist environment of the postwar years, Cabrales wrote to Peñarredonda: "The sad thing, my friend, is that Cubans, who are in no way similar to Anglo-Saxons, want to imitate them and listen to them in the race question, despite our very different condition. Cubans all, green or yellow, have sacrificed themselves for the fatherland and should all be united in its name."[16]

Cabrales's comment reveals the complex interaction between American and Cuban society. Throughout the many years of conflict with Spain, the United States' commitment to progress and democracy had served the rebels as a shining model. But when it came to racial politics, the United States, in the midst of a highly racist period, provided a poor example. Abandoning José Martí's vision of a republic of racial harmony, the new Cuban society, following in U.S. footsteps, soon made it clear that black Cubans, no matter how honorable their revolutionary pedigree, were not welcome. Women like María Cabrales and Elvira Bacardí, another widow of a black rebel, found that the best way to cope with the racial hostility of postwar Cuba was simply to withdraw from the public sphere. Cabrales explained to Peñarredonda: "I talked to Elvira, Bacardí's wife, two days ago. She said she received a letter from the capital appointing her the delegate of this town [Santiago] to collect funds to buy a house for Manana [Bernarda Toro, Máximo Gómez's wife]. She said she declined the noble offer to avoid the same difficulties I faced and which I mentioned to you. So it is, my dear friend, that evil has settled among us, dividing us when we should be most united to form our country, which has cost so many sacrifices and tears."[17] María Cabrales clearly understood that the exclusion of large sectors of Cuban society would make it difficult to successfully construct a new nation.

Despite its frustrating ending, the war brought changes that radically transformed Cuban society and Cuban womanhood. The American intervention opened many doors, both in schools and at work, for a new generation of Cuban women. After the war, women were able to get jobs as federal employees, telephone operators, and secretaries. Hundreds of women every year began to attend training schools to become teachers, and home economics schools multiplied.[18] The example of the Mambisas' courage inspired the women of the new republic to demand an expansion of their constitutional rights. Female activism resulted in a gradual improvement of women's status, marked by landmarks such as the 1918 divorce law and the suffrage law of 1934.[19]

All nationalist projects include the creation of myths and symbols that help cement the bond among disparate elements of society. The Mambisas' involvement in the anticolonial cause became a defining aspect of Cuba's historical memory and lore. The women's transgressions—their willingness to bend gender, class, and race conventions, to question traditions and to challenge authority—helped create a new identity for the Cuban people and pointed the way toward national unity. Yet the Mambisas' legacy is a conflicted one. The women's rebellion could be and has been used to defend the status quo, exhorting Cubans to put private concerns aside and make great sacrifices for the homeland. Similarly, the new sense of *cubanidad* redefined the ideal of femininity by celebrating women's strength, but also their adaptability and supportive role as good "*compañeras*" devoted to their family and their nation.

Reflecting its power, the symbol of the Mambisas was coveted and appropriated by all Cuban governments since the War of Independence, including the Castro regime. In the 1960s and the 1970s, socialist Cuba reclaimed several prominent figures, such as Evangelina Cossío Cisneros and Ana Betancourt, by bringing their remains to the Havana cemetery, where they were buried with full military honors. Embracing the Mambisas, the very symbol of nationhood, helped legitimize the revolutionary government. Lynn Stoner argues that the official rhetoric of Castro's Cuba highlights the Mambisas' combativeness, a convenient characteristic for a regime that demands from its people that they be ever militarily prepared.[20]

The woman warrior is an attractive image for contemporary sensibilities of both socialist and capitalist persuasions. Challenging traditional views about women's weakness and subordination, this image suits the contemporary tendency to celebrate female fitness, strength, and independence. The woman warrior works both as an erotic and a feminist icon. But I believe the real significance of the Mambisa's symbolism is a richer, more powerful one. Neither self-sacrificing assistant nor ferocious warrior, she stands, rather, as an icon of women who fought for political adulthood and citizenship.

Throughout the second half of the 1800s and in a long military confrontation, the Cuban people challenged Spain's colonial rule. Given the type of unconventional war this was, the role of the civilian population proved crucial to the survival of the insurgency. Women's contribution to the war effort was exceptional, a fact that was acknowledged by both the rebels and their enemies. Inspired by a strong attachment to their land and culture, and critical of the limitations the colonial system imposed, Cuban women fought and encouraged men to fight for freedom. Through their words and actions, they undermined conservative ideals and celebrated change. In the process, they helped create a new national identity and legitimized the notion that women had a role to play in Cuban politics.

Mambisas were passionately interested in the fate of their communities and were willing to confront their oppressive rulers. Their contributions stand as a testimony to women's ability to influence the course of history even when they lack formal authority.

Cuba's anticolonial wars, like all wars, brought death and destruction. But the fight against Spain also brought to Cuban women a new awareness of their power as historical agents.

Notes

Abbreviations

BNJM	Biblioteca Nacional José Martí
Rec. García mis.	Recortes García Miscelánea, BNJM
CC	Colección Cubana, BNJM
CM	Colección de Manuscritos, CC, BNJM
AHN	Archivo Histórico Nacional, Madrid
SU	Sección de Ultramar, AHN
ANRC	Archivo Nacional República de Cuba, Havana
PRC	Partido Revolucionario Cubano, ANRC

Introduction

1. O'Kelly, *The Mambi-Land*, 12–13.

2. Moreno Fraginals, *Cuba/España*, 291.

3. Ana Betancourt, "Datos biográficos."

4. See Stoner, "Militant Heroines," where the author analyzes the persistent use of the Mambisa as a nationalist icon from the nineteenth century to the present.

5. Franco, "Mariana y Maceo," 47.

6. Johnson, *Social Transformation*, 116.

7. Anderson, *Imagined Communities*, 6.

8. McClintock, *Imperial Leather*, 353.

9. See Gramsci, *Reader*.

10. Kutzinski, *Sugar's Secrets*, 17–42.

11. See Kerber, "History Can Do It No Justice," 4–5; Kristeva, *Reader*, 187–213.

12. For a provocative discussion of the fluidity of the concepts of gender and sex, see Butler, *Gender Trouble.*

13. Kaplan et al., *Between Women and Nation,* 12.

14. Stoner, "Militant Heroines," 79–87.

15. Helg, *Our Rightful Share.*

16. Johnson, "'Señoras en sus clases,'" 13.

17. Johnson, *Social Transformation,* 9.

18. For contrasting views on the cultural influence of Spain and the United States, see Moreno Fraginals, *Cuba/España,* and Pérez, *On Becoming Cuban.*

Chapter 1

1. Francisco Cabrera, *Misiva epistólica,* 12.

2. Raimundo Cabrera, *Cuba and the Cubans,* 265.

3. Villaverde, *Cecilia Valdés,* 180.

4. As reported in José M. Callejas's *Historia de Santiago de Cuba* (1911), after the Haitian revolution in 1791, fashionable girls in Santiago de Cuba benefited from an influx of French ladies who settled in their town and made a living by opening girls' academies. Quoted in Sarabia, *Historia,* 23.

5. Castillo, *Escritos,* 29–30.

6. Costales, *Educación de la mujer,* 69–73.

7. Quoted in Pérez, *Slaves, Sugar,* 182–87. See also Helg, *Our Rightful Share,* 25.

8. Valdés Mendoza, *Cantos perdidos,* 22.

9. Ibid., 28.

10. Rodríguez García, *De la revolución,* 69.

11. Castillo, "Carta al Sr. D. José Ramón de Betancourt."

12. Suárez y Romero, "Incompleta educación de las cubanas," 181–82.

13. Castillo, "Carta al Sr. D. José Ramón de Betancourt."

14. Ximeno, *Aquellos tiempos,* 21.

15. Quoted in Pérez, *Slaves, Sugar,* 13.

16. Ibid., 31.

17. Villaverde, *Cecilia Valdés,* 111.

18. Santa Cruz y Montalvo, *Viaje a la Habana,* 210.

19. Ibid., 206.

20. Ximeno, *Aquellos tiempos,* 4.

21. Ibid., 10.

22. Heredia, "Economía femenil," 78.

23. See Romero Tobar, "Los álbumes de las románticas," 73–93.

24. Borrero, *Poesías y cartas,* 89.

¡Por tus espaldas mórbidas / destrenza el rubio pelo; / deja extenderse indócil / el torrente de fuego / sobre tu seno túrgido / y el mármol de tu cuello!

25. Pérez de Zambrana, *Angélica y Estrella,* 102.

26. Pérez de Zambrana, *Antología,* 41–42.

Contestación

Y tú me dices, respetable amigo, / que me entregue al estudio noche y día, / que abra espacio a mi mente, que me eleve / en alas de la Hermosa poesía / a la etérea región, que abrace avara / la escena de los tiempos, que incansable / enaltezca mi ardiente fantasía / con objetos sublimes; que depure / mi gusto, y surque los inmensos, mares, / y abriendo mi alma a grandes impresiones / osada pise en extranjeros lares? /

Luego llevado de tu afecto dices / que la recompensa de mi afán un día / venturosa obtendré...mas ¡ay! amigo, / ¡Tú no pensaste que a tan hondo estudio / ingenio rico necesario fuera / y brillantes modelos? ¿Qué me falta / para poder enaltecer la mente / de esos objetos el aspecto grande / que no puedo admirar? ¿No te acordaste / al invitarme a recorrer naciones / que en el mundo implacable y malicioso / mujer, huérfana y joven nada puedo?

¡Oh y si supieras como mi alma ardiente / de emoción palpitante se recrea / con la embriagante y seductora idea / de ver abrirse las turgentes velas, / flotar el lino, levantarse el ancla, / crujir la quilla y como el viento raudo / volar meciéndose el bajel sereno / sobre la azul inmensidad...! ¡Dios mío! / Qué suprema ventura! ¡ Y yo no puedo /

Tanta dicha gozar... ¡Oh cuál extingue, / Cuál consume mi vida ese deseo / eterno, ardiente, inextinguible...! oh cielo! / Arranca, arranca por piedad del alma / esa ilusión irrealizable y loca, esa idea tenaz que me arrebata / la dulce paz que disfrutar ansío!

Mas perdona, perdona, amigo mío, / mi delirio febril; no a mí me culpes, / que esa frenética ansiedad me mata, / y sin poderla sofocar, eterna / bulle en mi mente y en mi seno vive.

Con lástima me miras... te comprendo.../ Te inspiro compasión... pues bien ¿lo sabes? /

Y no puedo ser nada, soy esclava / como mujer al fin, y el cuello doblo / Al yugo fuerte que nos priva injusto / de la adorable libertad que el hombre / goza feliz en su extensión eterna. / ¡Cuántas veces lloré con amargura / costumbre tan fatal...!

Mi buen amigo, / ya sabes cuánto se me opone y cuánto / yo lucho por vencer...! oh! no te ofendas / si a tu afectuosa invitación no cedo, / pues tú bien sabes que en el mundo injusto / mujer huérfana y joven nada puedo.

27. Gómez de Avellaneda, "Artículos," 5:292–93.
28. Ibid., 295.
29. Ibid., 306.
30. Quoted in Pérez de Zambrana, *Antología*, 136.

31. Gómez de Avellaneda, *Dos mujeres.*
32. Gómez de Avellaneda, *Sab*, 223.
33. Ibid., 129.
34. Suárez y Romero, *Francisco*, 41.
35. Castillo, *Escritos*, 116–17.
36. Ibid., 120–21; Castillo, "La mujer camagueyana."
37. Tanco Bosmeniel, *Petronila y Rosalía*, 104.
38. Ibid., 123.
39. Johnson, "Señoras en sus clases," 12–13.
40. Villaverde, *Cecilia Valdés*, 105–7.
41. Morúa Delgado, *Sofía*, 91.
42. See McClintock, *Imperial Leather*, 352–88.
43. Quoted in Pérez, *Cuba between Reform and Revolution*, 88.
44. Moreno Fraginals, *Cuba/España*, 281.
45. Caturla Bru, *La mujer*, 154.
46. Quoted in Zaragoza, *Las insurrecciones*, 1:171.

Chapter 2

1. Moreno Fraginals, *El ingenio*, 2:39. See also Scott, *Slave Emancipation,* and Pérez, *Cuba between Reform and Revolution.*
2. Villaverde, *Cecilia Valdés*, 194.
3. Pichardo, ed., *Documentos*, 1:331–40.
4. O'Kelly, *The Mambi-Land*, 64; Barcia, *La otra familia*, 154.
5. Moreno Fraginals, *El ingenio*, 2:53.
6. Pichardo, ed., *Documentos*, 1:333.
7. Zaragoza, *Las insurrecciones*, 2:696.
8. Barnet, *Biography of a Runaway Slave*, 38.
9. Ortiz, *Los negros esclavos*, 113. See also Moreno Fraginals, *El ingenio*, 2:44.
10. See contrasting views between Moreno Fraginals, *El ingenio,* and Rebecca Scott, *Slave Emancipation.*
11. Barnet, *Biography of a Runaway Slave*, 24.
12. Quoted in Moreno Fraginals, *El ingenio*, 2:43.
13. Castañeda Fuertes, "Demandas judiciales."
14. Barnet, *Biography of a Runaway Slave*, 32.
15. Ibid., 39.
16. Ortiz, *Los negros esclavos*, 155.
17. Ibid., 155–56.
18. See Paquette, *Sugar Is Made with Blood.*
19. Villaverde, *Cecilia Valdés*, 364; Barcia, *La otra familia*, 141.
20. Quoted in Ortiz, *Los negros esclavos*, 257.
21. Deschamps Chapeaux, "People without a History," 55.
22. Santa Cruz y Montalvo, *Viaje a la Habana*, 105.
23. Morillas, "El ranchador," 38–39.
24. Ibid., 43.

25. Barcia, *La otra familia*, 63.

26. Morúa Delgado, *Sofía*, 15–16.

27. Ibid., 18.

28. Helg, *Our Rightful Share*, 27–28. See also Martínez-Alier, *Marriage, Class, and Colour*, for how race shaped moral views of women.

29. Villaverde, *Cecilia Valdés*, 97.

30. Calcagno, *Romualdo*, 345

31. Martínez-Alier, *Marriage, Class, and Colour*, 53–54.

32. Ibid., 124–25.

Chapter 3

1. Quoted in Zaragoza, *Las insurrecciones*, 2:703 (Por Dios no salgáis de día/donde las gentes os vean;/pues por prudentes que sean/al ver trenzas o castañas/Os tendrán por alimañas/os silban, y os apedrean).

For God's sake don't go out in the daytime / where the people will see you; / for discreet as they may be / they will think you vermin / and will whistle and stone you.

2. Quoted in ibid., 701–2.

3. See Pérez, *Cuba between Reform and Revolution*, 83–84.

4. See Pérez, *Cuba and the United States*, 55–81. See also Poyo, "*With All*," 1–34.

5. Méndez Rodenas, *Gender and Nationalism*, 69–103.

6. Santa Cruz y Montalvo, *Viaje a la Habana*, 25. See also Araújo, *Viajeras al Caribe*, 130–144.

7. Gómez de Avellaneda, *Sab*, 74.

8. Agüero Estrada, *Biografía*, 7.

9. See Chaffin, *Fatal Glory*.

10. Agüero Estrada, *Biografía*, 11–12.

11. Pierra, "Insurrección."

12. Rec. García mis., no. 60.

De Libertad, Sublime y glorioso / el pendón recibid, camagüeyanos, / con entusiasmo desplegadlo, ufanos / que ha llegado el momento venturoso.

Haced que tremole siempre hermoso, / en vuestras firmes y valientes manos, / y el que ostentan los déspotas tiranos / destruid, con influjo portentoso.

Valientes . . . combatid . . . mientras al cielo / una plegaria alzamos fervorosa, / para que Dios nos de pronto el consuelo / de ver libre a nuestra patria Hermosa.

Combatid . . . combatid . . . que la Victoria / risueña os muestra el templo de la Gloria.

13. Morales y Morales, *Iniciadores*, 2:247–48.

14. Rec. García mis., nos. 61 and 189.

15. Calcagno, *Romualdo*, 290.

16. Morales y Morales, *Iniciadores*, 2:248

17. Rec. García mis., nos. 61 and 189.

18. Quesada y Miranda, *Ignacio Mora*, 22.

19. Pierra, "Insurrección."

20. Ibid.

21. Morales y Morales, *Iniciadores*, 2:249; see also Rec. García mis., nos. 61 and 189; and Lagomasinos, *Patricios y heroínas*, 33.

22. "Aquella Camagüeyana/que no se cortase el pelo/no es digna que en este suelo/la miremos como hermana" (Ponte Domínguez, *La mujer*, 9).

23. Portal, "Magdalena Peñarredonda."

Chapter 4

1. Scott, *Slave Emancipation*, 49.

2. Pichardo, ed., *Documentos*, 1:394–97.

3. AHN, SU, leg. 4343, no. 25.

4. AHN, SU, leg. 4348, no. 78.

5. Aguirre, *Influencia*, 68.

6. Quesada y Miranda, *Ignacio Mora*, 33.

7. Nuez González, *Mujeres en revolución*, 52–53.

8. Figueredo, *La abanderada*, 15.

9. Ibid., 16–17.

10. Caballero, *La mujer en el 68*, 69.

11. Anderson, *Imagined Communities*, 61–65.

12. Figueredo, *La abanderada*, 18–19.

13. Ibid., 19–20.

14. Ibid., 22.

15. Ibid., 26.

16. O'Kelly, *The Mambi-Land*, 183.

17. Ibid., 124.

18. Caballero, *La mujer en el 68*, 43–47.

19. Figueredo Socarrás, "Efemérides."

La Visita

En esta Sierra elevada / refugio de los cubanos / donde nunca los hispanos / pusieron su planta osada; / hay una loma enclavada / entre altísimas montañas, / donde entre flores y cañas, sin temores ni vigilia; / vive una honrada familia / bajo rústicas cabañas.

Allí la Revolución / con su impulso la arrojó / y desde entonces sintió / mejorar su situación. / Modelo de abnegación / y de santa fe cristiana. / En esta Guerra inhumana / que sostiene el despotismo / con ardiente patriotismo / sirve a la causa cubana.

A esta familia ligadas / puras, risueñas y hermosas, / hay seis niñas virtuosas, / Envidia sienten las hadas / Por su gracia y su primor; / pues vierte tanto esplendor / su belleza sin igual, / que en mi tierra tropical / son las reinas del Amor.

20. Rec. García mis., no. 187. See also Portal, "Concha Agramonte"; Ubieta, "Algunos datos biográficos," 388.

21. Lagomasinos, *Patricios y heroínas*, 120.

22. F. B. "Muerte."

23. Raúl Roa, *Aventuras*, 256.

24. Rec. García mis., no. 187.

25. See Anderson, *Imagined Communities*.

26. Quoted in Betancourt Agramonte, *Ignacio Agramonte*, 397.

27. Ibid., 204–5.

28. Agramonte Loynaz, *Patria y mujer*, 174–75.

29. Pirala y Criado, *Anales*, 1:635.

30. Ramón Roa, *Con la pluma*, 319.

31. See Ada Ferrer, *Insurgent Cuba*.

32. Arroyo, "Presencia de la mujer," 192.

33. Gómez y Toro, *Revoluciones*, 286–91.

34. Arroyo, "Presencia de la mujer," 192.

35. Rodríguez de Cuesta, *Patriotas cubanas*, 123–26.

36. Ubieta, "La mujer cubana."

37. Quoted in Sarabia, *Historia*, 48.

Si nace libre la hormiga, / la bibijagua y el grillo, / sin cuestiones de bolsillo / ni español que los persiga, / ninguna ley los obliga / a ir a la escribanía / a comprar la libertad, / y yo, con mi dignidad, / no sere libre algún día?

38. Stubbs, "Social and Political Motherhood," 306.

39. Sarabia, *Historia*, 78.

40. Rec. García mis., nos. 219, 221.

41. Martí, *Obras completas*, 5:26–27.

42. Elshtain, *Women and War*, 70.

43. Kerber, "History Can Do It No Justice," 22.

44. José Antonio Portuondo, ed., *Capítulos de literatura cubana*, 440.

45. Martí, *Obras completas*, 5:26.

46. Pirala y Criado, *Anales*, 1:745.

47. Cruz, *Episodios*, 198.

48. Ramón Roa, *A pie y descalzo*, 58–59.

49. Ibid., 63.

50. Cruz, *Episodios*, 18–25.

51. Pirala y Criado, *Anales*, 1:355.

52. AHN, SU, Cuba Gobierno, leg. 4340, no. 6.

53. Ibid., no. 24.

54. Ibid., leg. 4342, no. 8.

55. Ibid., leg. 4347, no. 23.
56. Ibid., leg. 4340, no. 6.
57. Ibid., no. 43.
58. Figueredo Socarrás, *La revolución*, 204.
59. Ramón Roa, *Con la pluma*, 257.
60. Cruz, *Episodios*, 157.
61. Rec. García mis., no. 217a.
62. Ramón Roa, *Con la pluma*, 181.
63. Ripley, *From Flag to Flag*, 236.
64. Pirala y Criado, *Anales*, 1:485.
65. Ramón Roa, *A Pie y descalzo*, 25.
66. Ibid., 18.
67. "Virgen de la Caridad/Divinísima señora/Te pedimos sin demora/De Cuba la Libertad"(ibid., 31).
68. Pirala y Criado, *Anales*, 1:635.

Chapter 5

1. *Apuntes biográficos*, 10.
2. Ibid., 10.
3. Ibid., 14–15.
4. Ibid., 29.
5. Ibid., 53.
6. Rodríguez García, *De la revolución*, 117.

El ímpetus marcial, Emilia, doma / No en cruenta lid tu noble ardor se invierta, / ¡Ah! no la mansa y tímida paloma / en fiero halcón de guerra se convierta!

7. *Apuntes biográficos*, 94–95.
8. Ibid., 76.
9. Ibid., 44.
10. Ibid., 53–55.
11. Ibid., 59.
12. Ibid., 60.
13. *Apuntes biográficos*, 107–8.
14. Ibid., 109–10.
15. Ibid., 148.
16. Ibid., 163–66.
17. Ibid., 176.
18. Rec. García mis., no. 202.
19. Quesada, *Ignacio Mora*, 37.
20. Betancourt, "Datos biográficos." Also in Rec. García mis., no. 194a.
21. Betancourt, "Datos biográficos."
22. Ibid.
23. Ibid. Gonzalo de Quesada presents a polished version of Ana Betancourt's words

in *Ignacio Mora*, 45. Quesada's version is the one Cuban historians always quote and the one that was translated into English. I have chosen to use the speech as remembered by Betancourt herself. While not as eloquent, her words have a ring of authenticity that Quesada's version lacks.

24. Betancourt, "Datos biográficos."
25. Quoted in Sarabia, *Ana Betancourt*, 86.
26. Castillo, *Escritos*, 37.
27. Quoted in Sarabia, *Ana Betancourt*, 87.
28. Ibid., 90.
29. Ibid.
30. Ibid.
31. Ibid., 93.
32. Rec. García mis. no. 194a.

Chapter 6

1. Caballero, *La mujer en el 95*. See also Rec. García mis., nos. 217a, 217b.
2. Quoted in Sarabia, *Historia*, 119.
3. Morales, *Iniciadores*, 3:261.
4. Morúa Delgado, *Sofía*, 59–60.
5. Ibid., 109.
6. Mendieta Costa, *Cultura*, 85–89.
7. Ramos, "La división."
8. Borrero, *Poesías y cartas*, 82.

¡No es posible! ¡Esperad! ¡quizás no tarde / de la batalla entre el confuso estruendo / de ¡Libertad! el anhelado grito / en conmover vuestros sagrados restos!

See also Rec. García mis., no. 196. Juana Borrero died of tuberculosis in 1896 in Key West, Florida, where her family had to take refuge to avoid political persecution. Only eighteen, she still left behind a rich and intriguing poetic legacy.

9. Quoted in García Yero, *La escritura*, 74–76.
10. Helg, *Our Rightful Share*, 26.
11. Scott, *Slave Emancipation*, 288.
12. Montejo Arrechea, "*Minerva*," 33–48.
13. Martí, *Obras completas*, 5:16–17.
14. Loynaz del Castillo, "La mujer cubana," 17.
15. Quoted in Sarabia, *Historia*, 102.
16. Ibid., 125.
17. *Patria*, October 6, 1893.
18. See Ferrer, *Insurgent Cuba*.
19. García Garcés, "El financiamiento."
20. Padrón, *La mujer trabajadora*, 5–7.

21. See Pedro Luis Padrón, *La mujer trabajadora.*

22. See Nancy Hewitt, *Southern Discomfort.*

23. Martí, *Obras completas,* 5:15–16.

24. Quesada, *Archivo,* 2:184.

25. Ibid., 185.

26. Mañach, *Martí,* 214.

27. Sociedad Política Cubana Hijas de Hatuey, Reglamento.

28. Borbón, *Cartas,* 34.

29. Ibid., 43.

30. Ibid., 49.

31. Ibid., 58.

Chapter 7

1. Ponte Domínguez, *La mujer,* 14.

Eterna Bordadora

I. Cuando se oyó el grito en Yara, / abandonando su hogar, / su esposo se fue a pelear, / el odio escrito en la cara.

Ella joven como era, / llena de entusiasmo santo, / bordó una rica bandera, / en la que envuelto volviera. / !muerto!, aquel que amara tanto.

II. El hijo heredó la fiera / ansía por la redención ; / con fervorosa pasíon, / ella bordó otra bandera.

¡Bandera que fue sudario / de aquel expedicionario / que, desplegándola al aire, / murió, mártir voluntario, / en un manigual de Baire!

III. En el antes dulce hogar, / La viuda infunde respeto. / ¡Cómo cuida de su nieto / que ha de saberse vengar! ...

Crece el niño, y ella espera / Que atienda Dios su plegaria / ¡verlo triunfar, o que muera! / con la estrella solitaria.

2. Portal, "Charito Bolaños."

3. Partido Revolucionario Cubano, "Club de Damas Clemencia Báez," Reglamento.

4. See Hewitt, *Southern Discomfort,* 71, 79–80, 107, 112, for a description of Fredesvinda Sánchez's and other women's activities.

5. Rec. García mis., no. 232. See also *Revista Cayo Hueso* (September 26, 1897), 14, 19; (December 26, 1897), 11.

6. Estrade, *Les clubs féminins,* 8.

7. Hewitt, *Southern Discomfort,* 74.

8. Caballero, *La mujer en el 95.*

9. ANRC, PRC, C-117-15-900 [ANRC, Partido Revolucionario Cubano-Caja (box) 117-(series number) 15-(document number) 900].

10. Castillo, *Escritos*, 39.

11. Caturla Bru, *La mujer*, 189.

12. Secades, "Defensa," 247.

13. Castellanos, "La manigua sentimental," in *Los argonautas, la manigua sentimental, cuentos.*

14. Franco, *Antonio Maceo*, 3:67.

15. Cabrales, *Epistolario*, 74.

16. Ibid., 76–77.

17. Ibid., 81.

18. Miró Argenter, *Crónicas*, 81–82.

19. Flint, *Marching with Gomez*, 6.

20. Franco, *Antonio Maceo*, 3:355.

21. Ibid., 240.

22. Ortiz, "Elogio póstumo a Marta Abreu," 96. See also Rec. García mis., no. 183.

23. CM, Abreu, nos. 22a, 22b.

24. Aguirre, *Influencia*, 85.

25. CM, Abreu, no. 314a(2).

26. Ibid., no. 314(2).

27. Rodríguez de Cuesta, *Patriotas cubanas*, 49–50. See also CM, Abreu, no. 44, and CM, Escoto, no. 236, for Eva Adán's description of the Camagüeyan women's trip to Las Recogidas.

28. CM, Arango, no. 17.

29. Ibid., no. 88.

30. New York *Journal* (February 12, 1897).

31. Brown, *The Correspondents' War*, 81.

32. Wilkerson, *Public Opinion*, 44.

33. CM, Arango, no. 82.

34. Ibid., no. 42.

35. Ibid., nos. 93, 54–58.

36. Rec. García mis., no. 218.

37. Franco, *Antonio Maceo*, 1:211.

38. ANRC, PRC, C-74, no. 13013-02.

39. Ibid.

40. Ibid., no. 13024.

41. CM, Peñarredonda, no. 4.

42. Ibid.

43. Portal, "Magdalena Peñarredonda."

44. Piedra Martel, *Memorias*, 38.

45. Boza, *Mi diario*, 43.

46. Fernando Gómez, *La insurrección*, 72.

47. Flint, *Marching with Gomez*, 257.

48. Elorza and Hernández Sandoica, *La guerra de Cuba*, 198.

49. Quoted in ibid., 195.

50. Franco, *Antonio Maceo*, 3:279.

51. Poumier, *Apuntes*, 132.

52. CM, Arango, no. 54.

53. Atkins, *Sixty Years in Cuba*, 276.

54. Ramiro Guerra, *Por las veredas*, 96.

55. Ibid., 104–5.

56. ANRC, PRC, C-74-13011.

57. Caballero, *La mujer en el 95*, 80–81.

58. Herrera, *Impresiones*, 120.

59. Rec. García mis., no. 203.

60. Flint, *Marching with Gomez*, 216–17.

61. Santovenia, *Huellas de gloria*, 198.

62. Ibid., 197; Portal, "Isabel Rubio."

63. Rec. García mis., no. 191.

64. Caballero, *La mujer en el 95*. See also Nuez González, ed., *Mujeres en revolución*.

65. Caballero, *La mujer en el 95*, 64.

66. Flint, *Marching with Gomez*, 87.

67. Rec. García mis., no. 235.

68. Piedra Martel, *Memorias*, 107–8.

69. Herrera, *Impresiones*, 58.

70. Martínez Moles, *Epítome*, 108–9.

71. Caballero, *La mujer en el 95*, 80–81.

72. Collazo, "De los tiempos," 8.

73. Castillo, *Escritos*, 173.

74. Ibid., 177.

75. Ibid., 179.

76. Quoted in García Yero, *La escritura*, 91–92.

77. Quoted in Armando Guerra, *Martí*, 30.

78. Ibid., 25.

79. Ibid., 37.

80. Hewitt, "The Voice."

81. Rec. García mis., nos. 215, 216.

82. Boza, *Mi diario*, 172–73.

83. Rodríguez Abascal, "Memoria," 146.

84. Camín in CM, Iraizoz, no. 14.

85. Iraizoz, CM, Iraizoz, no. 14

86. Poumier, *Apuntes*, 38.

Chapter 8

1. Rec. García mis., no. 208.

2. Ibid.

3. CM, Arango, no. 78.

4. New York *Journal* (October 10, 1897).

5. New York *World* (August 21, 1897).

6. Ibid.

7. Dunbar, *A Cuban Amazon*, 7.

8. Ibid., 92.

9. Ibid.

10. New York *Journal* (October 10, 1897). See Kristin Hoganson, *Fighting for American Manhood*, for a fascinating discussion on the intersection of gender and imperialism.

11. *Revista Cayo Hueso* (July 25, 1898), 15–16.

12. CM, Arango, no. 79; See Campbell, "Not a Hoax . . . ," for a detailed description of the involvement of the U.S. consulate personnel in Havana, including Rockwell, in the Cossío Cisneros case.

13. New York *Journal* (October 15, 1897).

14. *Revista Cayo Hueso* (September 26, 1897), 8.

15. Campbell, *Yellow Journalism*, 107–8.

16. New York *Journal* (October 10, 1897).

17. *The Story of Evangelina Cisneros*, 22.

18. New York *Journal* (October 18, 1897).

19. Ibid. (October 11, 1897).

20. Ibid. (October 15, 1897).

21. Ibid.

22. Ibid. (October 16, 1897).

23. Ibid.

24. Ibid.

25. Ibid. (October 18, 1897).

26. Ibid.

27. Ibid.

28. Ibid.

29. Albert, "The Rescue," 134.

30. Rec. García mis., no. 208.

31. Ibid.

32. Ibid.

Epilogue

1. García Yero, *La escritura*, 9.

2. Rec. García mis., no. 217c.

3. Rodríguez de Cuesta, *Patriotas cubanas*, 137–38.

4. F. B., "Muerte."

5. Smith and Padula, *Sex and Revolution*. See also Vinat, especially chapter 3.

6. Raúl Roa, *Aventuras*, 396.

7. *El Fígaro* (January 28, 1900), 41.

A Mi IIija

No tenemos hogar, hija del alma, / no tenemos hogar! / vamos así por el erial del mundo,/Sin asilo ni pan. / Sin una mano cariñosa y tierna / que apoye tu horfandad, / vamos tan solo recogiendo los abrojos / en el pobre cendal.

8. See Rodríguez de Cuesta, *Patriotas cubanas.*

9. ANRC, Fondo Máximo Gómez, leg. 35, no. 44 34 w-01.

10. Ibid., leg. 243182A-01.

11. Rec. García mis., no. 218.

12. ANRC, Donativos y Remisiones, leg. 94, 2 carta 02.

13. Ibid., 2 carta 03.

14. CM, Peñarredonda, no. 18.

15. Ibid., no. 9.

16. Ibid.

17. Ibid.

18. Smith and Padula, *Sex and Revolution*, 13. See also Miller, *Latin American Women*, 51.

19. See Stoner, *From the House to the Streets.*

20. Stoner, "Militant Heroines," 91–92.

Bibliography

Primary Sources

Archivo Nacional República de Cuba, Havana
Donativos y Remisiones
Fondo Máximo Gómez
Partido Revolucionario Cubano
Biblioteca Nacional José Martí, Havana
Colección de Manuscritos: Abreu, Arango, Borrero, Castillo, Iraizoz, Lufriu, Morales, Peña-
    rredonda, Ponce, and Treserra files, among others
Recortes García Miscelánea; also known as Colección Facticia Faustino García
Colección Cubana
Folletos
Archivo Histórico Nacional, Madrid
Sección de Ultramar. Cuba, Gobierno

Secondary Sources

Abel, Christopher, and Nissa Torrents. *José Martí: Revolutionary Democrat.* Durham, N.C.:
    Duke University Press, 1986.
Agramonte Loynaz, Ignacio. *Patria y mujer.* Havana: Cuaderno de Cultura, 1942.
Agüero Estrada, Francisco. *Biografía de Joaquín de Agüero y Agüero.* New York: N.p., 1853.
Aguirre, Mirta. *Influencia de la mujer en Iberoamérica.* Havana: Imprenta P. Fernández y
    Cía., 1947.
Albert, Kyle Hunter. "The Rescue of Evangelina Cisneros: While Others Talk the Journal
    Acts." M.A. thesis, University of Montana, 1984.
Álvarez Estévez, Rolando. *La emigración cubana en Estados Unidos, 1868–1878.* Havana:
    Editorial de Ciencias Sociales, 1986.

Anderson, Benedict. *Imagined Communities: Reflections on the Origin and Spread of Nationalism.* 1983. Revised edition. Verso: London, New York, 1996.

Apuntes biográficos de Emilia Casanova Villaverde escritos por un contemporáneo. New York: N.p., 1874.

Araújo, Nara, ed. *Viajeras al Caribe.* Havana: Casa de las Américas, 1983.

Arroyo, Anita. "Presencia de la mujer en la vida cubana." *Diario de la Marina,* número extraordinario (September, 1957): 192–99.

Atkins, Edwin F. *Sixty Years in Cuba.* 1926. Reprint. New York: Arno Press, 1980.

Azcuy Alón, Fanny. *El partido revolucionario y la independencia de Cuba.* Havana: Molina y Cía., 1930.

Bacardí y Moreau, Emilio. *Crónicas de Santiago de Cuba.* 3 vols. Santiago de Cuba: Tipografía Arroyo, 1923–25.

Barcia Zequeira, María del Carmen. *La otra familia. Parientes, redes y descendencia de los esclavos en Cuba.* Havana: Casa de las Américas, 2003.

Barnet, Miguel. *Biography of a Runaway Slave.* 1896. Reprint. Havana: Curbstone Press, 1994.

Betancourt, Ana. "Correspondencia, Memorias, etc." Colección de Manuscritos, Ponce, n. 365, Biblioteca Nacional José Martí.

———. "Datos biográficos de Ignacio Mora." Colección de Manuscritos, Morales, T. 37, no. 8m, Biblioteca Nacional José Martí.

Betancourt Agramonte, Eugenio. *Ignacio Agramonte y la revolución cubana.* Havana: Dorrbecker, 1928.

Boloña, Concepción. *La mujer en Cuba por Coralia.* Havana: Imprenta "La Prueba," 1899.

Borbón, Eulalia de. *Cartas a Isabel II: Mi viaje a Cuba y Estados Unidos.* Barcelona: Editorial Juventud, 1949.

Borrero, Juana. *Grupo de familia: Poesías de los Borrero.* Havana: Imprenta Moderna, 1895.

———. *Poesías y cartas: Juana Borrero.* Fina García Marruz and Cintio Vitier, eds. Havana: Editorial Arte y Literatura, 1978.

Boti, Regino. *Guillermón: Notas biográficas del General Guillermo Moncada.* Guantánamo: La Imparcial, 1911.

Boza, Bernabé. *Mi diario de guerra: Desde el baire hasta la intervención americana.* 2 vols. Havana: Imprenta "La Propagandista," 1905.

Brown, Charles H. *The Correspondents' War: Journalists in the Spanish-American War.* New York: Charles Scribner's Sons, 1967.

Butler, Judith. *Gender Trouble: Gender and the Subversion of Identity.* New York: Routledge, 1990.

Caballero, Armando. *La mujer en el 68.* Havana: Gente Nueva, 1978.

———. *La mujer en el 95.* Havana: Gente Nueva, 1983.

Cabrales, Gonzalo, ed. *Epistolario de héroes: Cartas y documentos históricos.* Havana: Siglo XX, 1922.

Cabrera, Francisco A. *Misiva epistólica: En defensa de la mujer cubana impugnando a Max Sibald.* Havana: Imprenta Mercantil de los Herederos de S. S. Spencer, 1885.

Cabrera, Raimundo. *Cuba and the Cubans.* Philadelphia: Levytype Company, 1896.

Cairo, Ana. "Emilia Casanova y la dignidad de la mujer cubana." *Revista Contracorriente* (July–August–September, 1997): 12–21.

Calcagno, Francisco. *Romualdo: Uno de tantos.* 1881. Reprint. In *Noveletas cubanas,* Imeldo Álvarez, ed., 278–386. Havana: Editorial Arte y Literatura, 1977.

Caldwell, Robert G. *The Lopez Expeditions to Cuba, 1848–1851.* Princeton, N.J.: Princeton University Press, 1951.

Camín, Alfonso. "Carta de Alfonso Camín a Antonio Iraizoz." *Coleccion Manuscritos*, Iraizoz, 14. Biblioteca Nacional José Martí.

Campbell, W. Joseph. "Not a Hoax: New Evidence in the *New York Journal's* Rescue of Evangeline Cisneros." *American Journalism* 19 (Fall 2002): 67–94.

———. *Yellow Journalism: Puncturing the Myths, Defining the Legacies*. Westport, Conn.: Praeger, 2001.

Carbonell, Néstor. *Próceres: Ensayos biográficos*. Special edition. Havana: Montalvo y Cárdenas, 1920.

Carbonell y Rivero, Néstor. *Tampa: Cuna del Partido Revolucionario Cubano*. Havana: Siglo XX, 1957.

Carbonell, Walterio. *Crítica: Cómo surgió la cultura nacional*. Havana: Ediciones Yaka, 1961.

Cartoons of the War of 1898 Foreign and American. Chicago: Belford, Middle Brook, 1898.

Casanova, Emilia. "Liga de las Hijas de Cuba. Contra Aldama." Colección Cubana, Folleto C. 91, no. 1, Biblioteca Nacional José Martí.

Castañeda Fuertes, Digna. "Demandas judiciales de las esclavas en el siglo XIX cubano." *Temas* 5(1996): 60–65.

Castellanos, Jesús. *Los argonautas, la manigua sentimental, cuentos*. Havana: Siglo XX, 1916.

Castillo, Aurelia. "Carta al Sr. D. José Ramón de Betancourt." Colección de Manuscritos, Castillo 31, Biblioteca Nacional José Martí.

———. *Escritos de Aurelia Castillo de González*. Havana: Siglo XX, 1918.

———. "Esperemos." Colección de Manuscritos, Castillo 37, 38, Biblioteca Nacional José Martí.

———. "La mujer camagüeyana." Colección de Manuscritos, Castillo 56, Biblioteca Nacional José Martí.

———. "La mujer cubana." Colección de Manuscritos, Castillo 28, Biblioteca Nacional José Martí.

Caturla Bru, Victoria. *La mujer en las guerras de la independencia de América*. Havana: Jesús Montero Editor, 1945.

Cepero Bonilla, Raúl. *Azúcar y abolición*. 1948. Reprint. Barcelona: Editorial Crítica, 1976.

Chaffin, Tom. *Fatal Glory: Narciso Lopez and the First Clandestine U.S. War against Cuba*. Charlottesville: University Press of Virginia, 1996.

Collazo, Enrique. "De los tiempos que fueron: La mujer en la Revolución." *La Discusión* (May 23, 1924): 8.

———. *Desde Yara hasta el Zanjón: Apuntaciones históricas*. 1893. Reprint. Havana: Instituto del Libro, 1967.

Consuegra, Isabel. *Mambiserías*. Havana: Editorial Trópico, 1930.

Cooper, Frederick, and Ann Laura Stoler, eds. *Tensions of Empire: Colonial Cultures in a Bourgeois World*. Berkeley & Los Angeles: University of California Press, 1997.

Costales, Manuel. *Educación de la mujer*. 1852. Reprint. 7th edition. Havana: Librería e Imprenta de Elías F. Casona, 1884.

Cruz, Manuel de la. *Episodios de la revolución cubana*. 1890. Reprint. Havana: Instituto del Libro, 1967.

Cudjoe, Selwyn R., ed. *Caribbean Women Writers: Essays from the First International Conference*. Wesley, Mass.: Calaloux Publications, 1990.

Cuevas, Ginés de. *Tipo de las habaneras: Influencia de estas en la sociedad, estado de su educación, mejoras que admite y medio de llevarlas a cabo*. Havana: Imprenta de M. Soler, 1848.

Deschamps Chapeaux, Pedro. "People without a History." In *AfroCuba: An Anthology of*

Cuban Writing on Race, Politics and Culture. Pedro Pérez Sarduy and Jean Stubbs, eds., 55–65. Melbourne: Ocean Press, 1993.

Dollero, Adolfo. *Cultura cubana.* Havana: Siglo XX de Aurelio Miranda, 1916.

Dunbar, Virginia Lyndall. *A Cuban Amazon.* Cincinnati, Ohio: Editor Publishing Company, 1897.

Elorza, Antonio, and Elena Hernández Sandoica. *La guerra de Cuba (1895–1898).* Madrid: Alianza Editorial, 1998.

Elshtain, Jean Bethke. *Women and War.* New York: Basic Books, 1987.

Estrade, Paul. *Les clubs féminins dans le Parti Revolutionnaire Cubain (1892–1898).* Paris: Publications de l'Equipe de Recherche de l'Université de PARIS VIII, 1986.

F. B. "Muerte de una patriota: La Sra. Concepción Agramonte vda. de Sánchez." *El Fígaro* (September 3, 1922): 575.

Fernández Robaina, Tomás. *Bibliografía de la mujer cubana.* Havana: Ministerio de Cultura, 1985.

Ferrer, Ada. *Insurgent Cuba: Race, Nation, and Revolution, 1868–1898.* Chapel Hill: University of North Carolina Press, 1999.

Figueredo, Candelaria. *La abanderada de 1868. Autobiografía. Candelaria Figueredo (hija de Perucho).* Havana: Cultural, 1929.

Figueredo Socarrás, Fernando. "Efemérides de la revolución." *La Discusión* (July 4, 1917): 10.

———. *La revolución de Yara, 1868–1898, conferencias.* 1902. Reprint. Havana: Instituto del Libro, 1968.

Flint, Grover. *Marching with Gomez: A War Correspondent's Field Note-Book Kept during Four Months with the Cuban Army.* 1898. Reprint. Boston: Houghton Mifflin, 1899.

Foner, Philip S. *The Spanish-Cuban-American War and the Birth of American Imperialism, 1895–1902.* 2 vols. New York: Monthly Review Press, 1972.

Franco, José Luciano. *Antonio Maceo: Apuntes para una historia de su vida.* 3 vols. 1951. Reprint. Havana: Editorial de Ciencias Sociales, 1975.

———. "Mariana y Maceo." In *Afrocuba: An Anthology of Cuban Writing, Politics and Culture,* Pedro Pérez Sarduy and Jean Stubbs, eds., 47–54. Melbourne: Ocean Press, 1993.

———. *Los palenques de los negros cimarrones.* Havana: Departamento de Orientación Revolucionaria del Comité Central del Partido Comunista de Cuba, 1973.

Gallenga, A. *The Pearl of the Antilles.* London: Chapman and Hall, 1873.

García, Faustino. "La mujer en la guerra." *Bohemia* (February 24, 1950): 80–84, 186–94.

García Garcés, Augusto. "El financiamiento de la guerra de independencia de Cuba, 1892–1898." Paper delivered at "A Cien Años del 98: Imperialismos, Revoluciones y Realidades de Fin de Siglo" Conference, June 21–July 21, 1998, Universidad de Oriente, Santiago de Cuba.

García Garófalo, Manuel. *Marta Abreu Arencibia y el Dr. Luis Estévez y Romero: Estudio biográfico.* Havana: Imprenta La Moderna Poesía, 1925.

García Marruz, Fina. *Juana Borrero: Estudio preliminar.* Havana: Editorial Arte y Literatura, 1966.

García Yero, Olga. *La escritura a conciencia: Aurelia Castillo, Una escritora olvidada.* Camagüey, Cuba: Editorial Acana, 2002.

Gómez, Fernando. *La insurrección por dentro: Apuntes para la historia.* 2nd edition. Madrid: Biblioteca de la Irradiación, 1900.

Gómez, Máximo. *Cartas a Francisco Carrillo*, Hortensia Pichardo, ed. Havana: Editorial de Ciencias Sociales, 1986.

Gómez de Avellaneda, Gertrudis. "Artículos sobre la condición de la mujer: Album de lo bello y de lo bueno." In *Obras literarias: Colección completa*. 5 vols. Madrid: Imprenta y Esterotipia de M. Rivadeneyra, 1871.

———. *Dos mujeres*. In *Obras de la Avellaneda*. 5 vols. Havana: Imprenta Aurelio Miranda, 1914.

———. *Sab*. Nina M. Scott, trans. and ed. Austin: University of Texas Press, 1993.

Gómez y Toro, Bernardo, ed. *Revoluciones . . . Cuba y hogar*. Havana: Imprenta de Rambla Bouza, 1927.

González Curquejo, Antonio. *Florilegio de escritoras cubanas*. Havana: Librería Imprenta la Moderna Poesía, 1910.

González Sedeño, Modesto. *La vida pública y secreta de encarnación de Varona*. Havana: Centro de Investigación y Desarrollo de la Cultura Cubana Juan Marinello, 2004.

Gramsci, Antonio. *The Gramsci Reader: Selected Writings 1916–1935*, David Forgacs, ed. New York: New York University Press, 2000.

Gray, Richard B. *José Martí: Cuban Patriot*. Gainesville: University of Florida Press, 1962.

Guerra, Armando. *Martí y la mujer: Conferencia*. Artemisa, Cuba: Editorial "El Pueblo," 1933.

Guerra, Ramiro. *Guerra de los 10 años*. 2 vols. Havana: Editorial de Ciencias Sociales, 1972.

———. *Por las veredas del pasado*. Havana: Editorial Lex, 1957.

Gutiérrez, Jose Margarito. *La mujer: Defensa de sus derechos e ilustración. Ensayo literario*. Key West, Fla.: Imprenta El Pueblo, 1886.

Hahner, June H. *The Struggle for Women's Rights in Brazil, 1850–1940*. Durham, N.C.: Duke University Press, 1990.

Helg, Aline. *Our Rightful Share: The Afro-Cuban Struggle for Equality, 1886–1912*. Chapel Hill: University of North Carolina Press, 1995.

Heredia, José María. "Economía femenil." In *Cuentos cubanos del siglo XIX: Antología*, Salvador Bueno, ed. Havana: Editorial Arte y Literatura, 1975.

Herrera, José Isabel. *Impresiones de la guerra de la independencia (narrado por el soldado del Ejército Libertador José Isabel Herrera (Mangoche)*. Havana: Editorial Nuevos Rumbos, 1948.

Hewitt, Nancy. "Compounding Differences." *Feminist Studies* 18, no. 2 (Summer, 1992): 313–26.

———. "Paulina Pedroso and las Patriotas de Tampa." In *Spanish Pathways in Florida, 1492–1992*, Ann Henderson and Gary Mormino, eds., 258–79. Sarasota, Fla.: Pineapple Press, 1991.

———. *Southern Discomfort: Women's Activism in Tampa*. Urbana: University of Illinois Press, 2001.

———. "The Voice of Virile Labor: Labor Militancy, Community Solidarity, and Gender Identity among Tampa's Latin Workers, 1880–1921." In *Work Engendered: Toward a New History of American Labor*, Ava Baron, ed., 142–67. Ithaca, N.Y.: Cornell University Press, 1991.

Hoganson, Kristin. *Fighting for American Manhood: How Gender Politics Provoked the Spanish-American and Philippine-American Wars*. New Haven, Conn.: Yale University Press, 1998.

Horrego Estuch, Leopoldo. *Emilia Casanova: La vehemencia del separatismo: Trabajo leído por Leopoldo Horrego Estuch en sesión pública el día 16 de marzo de 1951.* Havana: Siglo XX, 1951.

Ibarra, Jorge. *Ideología mambisa.* Havana: Instituto del Libro, 1967.

Iraizoz, Antonio. "La Heroína de Paso real." *Colección Manuscritos,* Iraizoz, 14. Biblioteca Nacional José Martí.

Iznaga, Diana. *Presencia del testimonio en la literatura sobre las guerras de la independencia nacional: 1868–1898.* Havana: Editorial Letras Cubanas, 1989.

Jiménez Pastrana, Juan. *Los chinos en las luchas por la liberación cubana, 1847–1930.* Havana: Instituto de Historia, 1963.

Johnson, Sherry. "'Señoras en Sus Clases No Ordinarias.' Enemy Collaborators or Courageous Defenders of the Family?" *Cuban Studies* 34 (2003): 11–37.

———. *The Social Transformation of Eighteenth-Century Cuba.* Gainesville: University Press of Florida, 2001.

Kaplan, Caren, Norma Alarcón, and Minoo Moallem, eds. *Between Women and Nation: Nationalism, Transnational Feminism, and the State.* Durham, N.C.: Duke University Press, 1999.

Kerber, Linda K. "History Can Do It No Justice: Women and the Reinterpretation of the American Revolution." In *Women in the Age of the American Revolution,* Ronald Hoffman and Peter J. Albert, eds., 3–42. Charlottesville: University Press of Virginia, 1989.

Kirkpatrick, Susan. *Las románticas: Escritoras y subjetividad en España, 1835–1850.* Madrid: Ediciones Cátedra, 1989.

Knight, Franklin W. *Slave Society in Cuba during the Nineteenth Century.* Madison: University of Wisconsin Press, 1970.

Kristeva, Julia. *The Kristeva Reader,* Toril Moi, ed. New York: Columbia University Press, 1986.

Kutzinski, Vera M. *Sugar's Secrets: Race and the Erotics of Cuban Nationalism.* Charlottesville: University Press of Virginia, 1993.

LaFeber, Walter. *Inevitable Revolutions: The United States in Central America.* New York: Norton, 1984.

Lagomasinos, Luis A. *Patricios y heroínas: Bocetos históricos.* Havana: Siglo XX, 1912.

Linderman, Gerald F. *The Mirror of War: American Society and the Spanish-American War.* Ann Arbor: University of Michigan Press, 1974.

Loynaz del Castillo, E. "La mujer cubana." In *Epistolario de héroes: Cartas y documentos históricos coleccionados por Gonzalo Cabrales.* Havana: Siglo XX, 1922.

Lubow, Arthur. *The Reporter Who Would Be King: A Biography of Richard Harding Davis.* New York: Charles Scribner's Sons, 1992.

Mañach, Jorge. *Martí el apóstol.* 1942. Reprint. Madrid: Espasa Calpe, 1972.

Marquina, Rafael. "Ana Betancourt de Mola, heroína, patriota y primera feminista cubana." *Informaciones* (August 26, 1945): 4.

Martel Piedra, Manuel. *Memorias de un mambí.* Havana: Instituto del Libro, Colección Cocuyo, 1968.

Martí, José. *Obras completas.* 27 vols. Havana: Editorial Nacional de Cuba, 1963–66.

Martínez-Alier, Verena (Stolcke). *Marriage, Class, and Colour in Nineteenth Century Cuba: A Study of Racial Attitudes and Sexual Values in a Slave Society.* 1974. Reprint. Ann Arbor: University of Michigan Press, 1989.

Martínez Moles, Manuel. *Epítome de la historia de Sancti Spíritu: Desde el descubrimiento de sus costas hasta nuestros días.* Havana: Boletín Nacional de Historia y Geografía, 1949.

McClintock, Anne. *Imperial Leather: Race, Gender and Sexuality in the Colonial Context.* New York: Routledge, 1995.

Méndez Rodenas, Adriana. *Gender and Nationalism in Colonial Cuba: The Travels of Santa Cruz y Montalvo, Condesa de Merlín.* Nashville, Tenn.: Vanderbilt University Press, 1998.

Mendieta Costa, Raquel. *Cultura: Lucha de clases y conflicto racial, 1878–1895.* Havana: Editorial Pueblo y Educación, 1989.

———. "De la isla a la nación: Otra opinión acerca de la nacionalidad cubana." *Temas* (Spring, 1990): 15–29.

Miller, Francesca. *Latin American Women and the Search for Social Justice.* Hanover, N.H.: University Press of New England, 1991.

Milton, Joyce. *The Yellow Kids: Foreign Correspondents in the Heyday of Yellow Journalism.* New York: Harper & Row, 1989.

Miró Argenter, José. *Crónicas de la guerra: Las campañas de invasión de occidente.* 3 vols. in one. 1909. Reprint. Havana: Editorial de Ciencias Sociales, 1970.

Momsen, Janet, ed. *Women and Change in the Caribbean: A Pan-Caribbean Perspective.* Bloomington: Indiana University Press, 1993.

Montejo Arrechea, Carmen. "*Minerva*: A Magazine for Women (and Men) of Color." In *Between Race and Empire: African-Americans and Cubans before the Cuban Revolution,* Lisa Brock and Digna Castañeda Fuertes, eds., 33–48. Philadelphia: Temple University Press, 1998.

Morales y Morales, Vidal. *Iniciadores y primeros mártires de la revolución cubana.* 3 vols. 1901. Reprint. Havana: Colección de Libros Cubanos, 1931.

Moreno Fraginals, Manuel. *Cuba/España, España/Cuba: Historia común.* Barcelona: Crítica, 1995.

———. *El ingenio: Complejo económico-social cubano del azúcar.* 3 vols. Havana: Editorial de Ciencias Sociales, 1978.

Morillas, Pedro José. "El ranchador." In *Noveletas cubanas,* Imeldo Álvarez, ed., 21–44. Havana: Editorial de Arte y Literatura, 1977.

Mormino, R. Gary, and George E. Pozetta. *The Immigrant World of Ybor City: Italians and Their Latin Neighbors in Tampa, 1885–1985.* Urbana: University of Illinois Press, 1987.

Morúa Delgado, Martín. *Sofía.* Reprint. Havana: Publicaciones de la Comisión Nacional del Centenario de Don Martín Morúa Delgado, 1957.

Muecke Bertel, Carlos. *Patria y libertad: En defensa del ejército libertador de Cuba como aliado de los americanos en 1898.* Camagüey, Cuba: Ramentol y Boan, 1928.

Musgrave, George C. *Under Three Flags in Cuba: A Personal Account of the Cuban Insurrection and the Spanish-American War.* Boston: Little, Brown, 1899.

Nelan, Charles. *Cartoons of Our War with Spain.* 2nd edition. New York: Frederick A. Stokes, 1898.

Norton, Mary Beth. *Liberty's Daughters: The Revolutionary Experience of American Women, 1750–1800.* Boston: Little, Brown, 1980.

Nuez González, Ada de la, ed. *Mujeres en revolución.* 1974. Reprint. Havana: Editorial de Ciencias Sociales, 1978.

O'Kelly, James J. *The Mambi-Land or Adventures of a Herald Correspondent in Cuba.* Philadelphia: J. B. Lippincott, 1874.

Olivares, José de. *Our Islands and Their People as Seen with Camera and Pencil.* 2 vols. New York: N. D. Thompson, 1899.

Ortiz, Fernando, ed. *Contra la anexión: José Antonio Saco*. Havana: Editorial Ciencias Sociales, 1974.

———. "Elogio póstumo a Marta Abreu por Fernando Ortiz. Pronunciado en la Sociedad Económica de Amigos del País el 9 de enero de 1920." *Revista Bimestre* (March–April, 1912): 91–99.

———. *Los negros esclavos*. 1916. Reprint. Havana: Editorial de Ciencias Sociales, 1996.

Padrón, Pedro Luis. *La mujer trabajadora*. N.p., 1972.

Padrón Valdés, Abelardo. *Guillermón Moncada: Vida y hazañas de un general*. Havana: Editorial Arte y Literatura, 1980.

Paquette, Robert L. *Sugar Is Made with Blood: The Conspiracy of La Escalera and the Conflict between Empires over Slavery in Cuba*. Middletown, Conn.: Wesleyan University Press, 1998.

Partido Comunista de Cuba. *La mujer cubana en los cien años de lucha: 1868–1968*. Havana: n.p., 1969.

Partido Revolucionario Cubano. "Club de Damas Clemencia Báez." Reglamento. Santo Domingo: Imprenta "Cuna de América," 1897.

Pérez, Louis A., Jr. *Cuba and the United States: Ties of Singular Intimacy*. Athens: University of Georgia Press, 1990.

———. *Cuba between Empires, 1878–1902*. Pittsburgh: University of Pittsburgh Press, 1988.

———. *Cuba between Reform and Revolution*. New York: Oxford University Press, 1995.

———. *On Becoming Cuban: Identity, Nationality and Culture*. Chapel Hill: University of North Carolina Press, 1999.

———, ed. *Slaves, Sugar and Colonial Society: Travel Accounts of Cuba, 1801–1899*. Wilmington, Del.: Scholarly Resources, 1992.

———. *The War of 1898: The United States and Cuba in History and Historiography*. Chapel Hill: University of North Carolina Press, 1998.

Pérez de la Riva, Juan. *El barracón y otros ensayos*. Havana: Editorial de Ciencias Sociales, 1975.

Pérez de Zambrana, Luisa. *Angélica y Estrella*. Havana: Escuela Nueva, 1957.

———. *Antología poética*. Havana: Editorial Arte y Literatura, 1977.

Pichardo, Hortensia, ed. *Documentos para la historia de Cuba*. 5 vols. Havana: Editorial de Ciencias Sociales, 1968–80.

———, ed. *Máximo Gómez: Cartas a Francisco Carrillo*. Havana: Editorial de Ciencias Sociales, 1986.

Piedra Martel, Manuel. 1943. Reprint. *Memorias de un mambí*. Havana: Instituto del Libro, 1968.

Pierra, Adolfo. "Insurrección de Joaquín de Agüero." February, 1902. Colección de Manuscritos, Lufriu, no. 4, Biblioteca Nacional José Martí.

Pirala y Criado, Antonio. *Anales de la guerra de Cuba*. 3 vols. Madrid: F. González Rojas, 1895–98.

Ponte Domínguez, Francisco. *Historia de la guerra de los diez años (hasta Guáimaro)*. Havana: Siglo XX, 1945.

———. *La mujer en la revolución cubana*. Havana: Molina, 1933.

Portal, Herminia del. "Las mambisas: Charito Bolaños." *Bohemia* (November 29, 1942): 20–21, 57–58.

———. "Las mambisas: Charito Morales de los Reyes." *Bohemia* (October 25, 1942): 6–7, 59–61.

———. "Las mambisas: Concha Agramonte." *Bohemia* (May 9, 1943): 14–15, 48, 68–69, 72.

———. "Las mambisas: Isabel Rubio." *Bohemia* (November 15, 1942): 4–5, 65, 68.

———. "Las mambisas: Magdalena Peñarredonda." *Bohemia* (December 13, 1942): 12–13, 60, 64–65.

Portuondo, Fernando. *Historia de Cuba, 1492–1898.* Havana: Editorial Pueblo y Educación, 1965.

Portuondo, José Antonio. *Capítulos de literatura cubana.* Havana: Editorial de Letras Cubanas, 1981.

Poumier, María. *Apuntes sobre la vida cotidiana en Cuba en 1898.* Havana: Editorial de Ciencias Sociales, 1975.

Poyo, Gerald E. *"With All and for the Good of All": The Emergence of Popular Nationalism in the Cuban Communities of the United States, 1848–1898.* Durham, N.C.: Duke University Press, 1989.

Procter, Ben. *William Randolph Hearst: The Early Years 1863–1910.* New York: Oxford University Press, 1998.

Quesada y Miranda, Gonzalo de. *Archivo de Gonzalo de Quesada, epistolario.* 2 vols. Havana: Academia de la Historia de Cuba, 1948.

———. *Ignacio Mora.* New York: Imprenta "América," 1984.

Ramos, Miguel W. "La División de la Habana: Territorial Conflict and Cultural Hegemony in the Followers of Oyo Lukumí Religion, 1850s–1920s." *Cuban Studies* 34 (2003): 38–70.

Ripley, Eliza McHattan. *From Flag to Flag: A Woman's Adventures and Experiences in the South during the War, in Mexico, and in Cuba.* New York: D. Appleton, 1889.

Roa, Ramón Mauricio. *A pie y descalzo: De Trinidad a Cuba, 1870–1871. Recuerdos de campaña.* Havana: Establecimiento Tipografía, 1890.

———. *Con la pluma y el machete.* 3 vols. Havana: Instituto del Libro, 1969.

Roa, Raúl. *Aventuras, venturas y desventuras de un mambí.* Havana: Editorial de Ciencias Sociales del Instituto del Libro, 1970.

Rodríguez Abascal, Pedro. "Memoria de 2 patriotas." *Bohemia* (August 20, 1950): 123, 144–46.

Rodríguez Calderón, Mirta, "Evangelina Cosío, la muchacha quinceañera," *Bohemia* 29 (July 21, 1967): 167–22.

Rodríguez de Cuesta, Vicentina. *Patriotas cubanas.* Pinar del Río, Cuba: Talleres "Heraldo Pinareño," 1952.

Rodríguez de Tío, Lola. *Mi libro de Cuba: Poesías.* Barcelona: Ediciones Rumbos, 1967.

Rodríguez García, José. *De la revolución y de las cubanas en la época revolucionaria: Discurso.* Havana: Siglo XX, 1930.

Romero Tobar, Leonardo. "Los álbumes de las románticas." In *Escritoras románticas españolas*, Marina Mayoral, ed., 73–93. Madrid: Fundación Banco Exterior, 1990.

Santa Cruz y Montalvo, Mercedes. *Mis doce primeros años.* 1905. Reprint. Havana: Siglo XX, 1922.

———. *Viaje a la Habana.* Havana: Editorial de Arte y Literatura, 1974.

Santovenia, Emeterio S. *Huellas de gloria: Frases históricas cubanas.* 1928. Reprint. Havana: Editorial Trópico, 1944.

———. *Mártires de la patria: Biografía de la patriota pinareña Isabel Rubio, capitana de sanidad del ejército libertador.* Havana: Editorial Trópico, 1913.

Sarabia, Nydia. *Ana Betancourt Agramonte.* Havana: Editorial de Ciencias Sociales, 1970.

———. *Historia de una mambisa: Mariana Grajales*. Havana: Instituto Cubano del Libro; Editorial Orbe, 1975.

———. *María Cabrales*. Havana: Gente Nueva, 1976.

Scott, Rebecca. *Slave Emancipation in Cuba: The Transition to Free Labor, 1860–1899*. Princeton, N.J.: Princeton University Press, 1985.

Secades, Manuel. Dissertation. "Defensa de los derechos de la mujer y de la prole en las uniones ilegítimas." Havana: Tipografía de "El Fígaro," 1903.

Shepherd, Verene, Bridget Brereton, and Barbara Bailey, eds. *Engendering History: Caribbean Women in Historical Perspective*. New York: St. Martin's Press, 1995.

Smith, Lois M., and Alfred Padula. *Sex and Revolution: Women in Socialist Cuba*. New York: Oxford University Press, 1996.

Sociedad Política Cubana Hijas de Hatuey, Reglamento. Santo Domingo. Colección Cubana, Folleto C. 398, no. 15, Biblioteca Nacional José Martí.

Stephens, Lynn. "Women in Mexico's Popular Movements against Ecological and Economic Impoverishment." *Latin American Perspectives* (Winter, 1992): 73–96.

Stern, Steve J. *Women, Men, and Power in Late Colonial Mexico*. Chapel Hill: University of North Carolina Press, 1995.

Stiff, Carol Wilcox. "Cuba's 'Gently Bred Revolutionary': Perspectives of the Spanish-Language Press, a Study of U.S., Cuban, and Spanish Coverage of the 1897 Prison Escape of Evangelina Cossío y Cisneros." Ph.D. dissertation, University of North Carolina at Chapel Hill, 2003.

Stoner, K. Lynn. *From the House to the Streets: The Cuban Woman's Movement for Legal Reform, 1898–1940*. Durham, N.C.: Duke University Press, 1991.

———. "Militant Heroines and the Consecration of the Patriarchal State: The Glorification of Loyalty, Combat, and National Suicide in the Making of Cuban National Identity." *Cuban Studies* 34 (2003): 71–96.

———. *The Women's Movement in Cuba, 1898–1958: The Stoner Collection on Cuban Feminism*. Wilmington, Del.: Scholarly Resources, 1991. Microform.

Stoner, K. Lynn, and Hipólito Serrano Pérez, eds. *Cuban and Cuban-American Women: An Annotated Bibliography*. Wilmington, Del.: Scholarly Resources, 2000.

The Story of Evangelina Cisneros Told by Herself: Her Rescue by Karl Decker. Julian Hawthorne, intro. New York: Continental Publishing, 1897.

Stubbs, Jean. "Social and Political Motherhood of Cuba: Mariana Grajales Cuello." In *Engendering History: Caribbean Women in Historical Perspective*. Verene Shepherd, Bridget Brereton, and Barbara Bailey, eds., 296–317. New York: St. Martin's Press, 1995.

Suárez y Romero, Anselmo. *Colección de artículos*. Havana: Establecimiento Tipografía "La Antilla," 1859.

———. *Francisco: El ingenio o las delicias del campo*. Havana: Editorial Pueblo y Educación, 1985.

———. "Incompleta educación de las cubanas." In *Artículos de costumbres cubanos del siglo XIX: Antología*, Iraida Rodríguez, ed., 181–91. Havana: Editorial de Arte y Literatura, 1974.

Tanco Bosmeniel, Félix M. *Petronila y Rosalía*. In *Cuentos cubanos del siglo XIX: Antología*, Salvador Bueno, ed., 103–31. Havana: Editorial Arte y Literatura, 1975.

Tejera, Diego. "La mujer cubana." Talk delivered at "Club Cubano de Cayo Hueso," February 15, 1898. Havana: Imprenta El Fígaro, 1899.

Twinam, Ann. *Public Lives, Private Secrets: Gender, Honor, Sexuality and Illegitimacy in Colonial Spanish America.* Stanford, Calif.: Stanford University Press, 1999.

Ubieta, Enrique. "Algunos datos biográficos de la Sra. Concepción Agramonte Vda. de Sánchez." In *Efemérides de la revolución cubana* (April, 1920): 388.

———. "Efemérides de la revolución." *El Fígaro* (September 3, 1922): 575.

———. "La mujer cubana en la revolución." *Bohemia* (December 24, 1910): 394.

Valdés Mendoza, Mercedes. *Cantos perdidos: Cartas sobre la educación del bello sexo (a las que se han añadido el compendio de moral y economía doméstica aplicado a las niñas, escrito por Juan Francisco Chaple): Obra declarada TEXTO para las escuelas públicas.* Havana: Imprenta y Librería de A. Pego, 1871.

Villaverde, Cirilo. *Cecilia Valdés o La loma del ángel.* 1882. Reprint. Havana: Editorial Letras Cubanas, 1977.

Vinat de la Mata, Raquel. *Las Cubanas en la posguerra (1898–1902). Acercamiento a la reconstrucción de una etapa olvidada.* Havana: Editorial Política, 2001.

Wilkerson, Marcus M. *Public Opinion and the Spanish American War: A Study in War Propaganda.* New York: Russell & Russell, 1932.

Wisan, Joseph. *The Cuban Crisis as Reflected in the New York Press, 1895–1898.* 1934. Reprint. New York: Octagon Books, 1965.

Ximeno, Dolores María de. *Aquellos tiempos . . . memorias de Lola María de Ximeno.* Colección Cubana de Libros y Documentos Inéditos o Raros, Fernando Ortiz, ed. 2 vols. Havana: "El Universo," 1928.

Zacharie de Baralt, Blanca. *El Martí que yo conocí.* Havana: Editorial Trópico, 1945.

Zaragoza, Justo. *Las insurrecciones en Cuba.* 2 vols. Madrid: Imprenta de Manuel G. Hernández, 1872–73.

Zayas, Alfredo. *La mujer y la revolución cubana.* Havana: Molina, 1942.

Index

Montejo Arrechea, Carmen, 93
Mora, Ignacio, 82–83, 85, 86
Morales, Ana, 70–71
Morales, María, 112
Morales, Raquel, 112
Morales, Rosario, 112
Morality: of slavery, 22; of soldiers, 61; of
    women, 15
Moreno Fraginals, Manuel, 8, 156n10
Moret law, 49
Morillas, Pedro José, 33
Morúa Delgado, Martín, 90
Mulata, 36
Music, 31

Napoleonic era, 39
Nationalism, 5, 58, 90, 92, 105, 151
Newspapers: American coverage of Cuban
    events, 112–13; revolutionary, 51, 65, 77,
    83; yellow press, 137–46. *See also names
    of specific newspapers*
New York *Journal* (newspaper), 112–13, 115,
    126, 137, 138, 140, 142–45
New York *World* (newspaper), 113, 115, 137,
    140
Niñas Cubanas y Portorriqueñas (Cuban and
    Puerto Rican Girls), 104
Noriega, Luz, 134–36
Nurses, 71–72, 94, 103, 112, 126–29

Obreras de la Independencia, 98
Occupation: of Cuba, 145
O'Kelly, James, 29, 54
Oriente: slavery in, 27–28
Ortiz, Fernando, 32
Oshun (goddess), 91
Our Lady of Charity, 91

Pact of Zanjón, 87, 88, 89, 92, 120
Padula, Alfred, 148
Palenque, 33, 34, 75
Palomares, Luz, 147
Pamphlets, 43, 83
Partido Revolucionario Cubano (Cuban
    Revolutionary Party), 93–94, 104, 112
Patriarchal society, 24
Patrocinados, 92

Pedroso, Paulina, 98
Pedroso, Ruperto, 98
Pelonas, 39
Peñarredonda, Magdalena: angered at revolu-
    tionary outcome, 149; as courier, 114–17;
    cutting hair as protest, 47, 114; photo of,
    117; on *reconcentración*, 124–25
Peninsulares, 41
Pérez, Bélen, 70
Pérez, Louis, 8
Pérez de Zambrana, Luisa, 17–19, 154n26
Petronila and Rosalía (Tanco), 23
Piedra Martel, Manuel, 130–31
Pierra, Adolfo, 43, 46
Pierra, Martina, 43
Pirala, Antonio, 69
Plantation society, 3, 4, 18, 27, 38, 48. *See also*
    Slavery
Platt Amendment, 145
Political prisoners, 111
Ponte Domínguez, Francisco, 162n1
PRC. *See* Cuban Revolutionary Party
Prefectos, 106, 119
Pregnant women: treatment of, 29, 32
Property: restoration of, 70
Puerto Principe, 46
Pulitzer, Joseph, 137
Punishment: for antigovernment activity,
    70; of slaves, 32

Quesada, Anita, 80
Quesada y Miranda, Gonzalo, 50, 160n23
Quinine, 126

Racial interaction, 37
Racism, 96, 150
"El ranchador" (Morilla), 33
El Ranchito, 54, 55
Rape: by soldiers, 106
Las Recogidas, 111–12, 149
Reconcentración, 120, 121–26, 136, 138
Reglamento de Esclavos (1842): children
    remaining with mothers, 31; marriage
    among slaves, 29–30; newborn infants,
    treatment of, 29; physical punishment
    of slaves, 32; work hours of slaves,
    28–29

Teresa Prados-Torreira is professor of history and cultural studies at Columbia College Chicago. She is currently working on a book about political satire.